Growing a Life of Prayer

a Workbook Journal
Including "Collection of Grace"

by Carrie Soukup

Mark it up!
Don't be afraid to scribble,
color, fold, or highlight!

Collection of Grace

ISBN: 9798669400644
Independently Published

For more copies of this book go to Amazon.com
Or, to purchase in bulk, please email GraceFinders.Carrie@gmail.com

Dedicated to Rosanne and Joanne
who have buoyed this project
and whose names happen to rhyme.

And of course, to my family.

Collection of Grace

Note to teachers-

Thank you so much for sharing yourself with students. It is not easy to be vulnerable and witness about your own relationship with God.

The goal of this book is to help readers thrive through a growing habit of prayer.

Many of the activities contained in this book are very personal – too personal for compelled sharing with a teacher or other students. Although it is a workbook, it is meant to parallel God's free invitation which Christ extends to each of us. I hope your experience with this book includes much flexibility and generosity both for your students and for yourself.

Table of Contents

Introduction to the Reader

Welcome, Friend! Today, you are invited to a deep relationship with God. You are invited to thrive everywhere. You are invited to self-knowledge, to take hold of the riches of the church, to purpose, to transformation and to community. In essence, you are welcomed to prayer. Where ever you are in life, however you feel right now is the perfect starting point. You might be far from God, or familiar with religious prayer, or confused, or on fire. No matter what, you are invited to the next step. God takes the initiative. He first walks to you and invites you to walk with him. There is no greater joy I personally have experienced than the life of God within and around me – an experience all are invited to. You are welcome to explore and see what comes of this. I am on my knees for you in this journey.

__What is this book?__ This is a resource book for a life of prayer which is somewhat systematic and comprises many aspects of life. This thorough life of prayer, is completely flexible to the movement of the Holy Spirit, the stage of development you are in, your circumstances, personality and desires. In here you will find an approach to life – prayers, explanations and tiny stories which help you to feel and experience the rhythm of continually turning to Jesus Christ and living in the Spirit.

The inner portion of this book - in standard black text - is the resource itself – the prayers and patterns which help to grow an inner life with God. Originally, this book only contained these resources but now, this edition contains activities to help you engage with the types of prayer in each chapter.

If you are anything like my kids, you will go straight to the activities in the grayed margin section – the checkboxes, fill in the blanks and line connections – and after filling it out, feel "done". However, the meat is in the middle. __Do a close read of the pages and prayers, then play in the margin with the activities.__

It does not stop there. Mark it up so you can daily use the texts and prayers for your conversation with God. Journal in the margins so you can remind yourself of the ideas and dreams you have along the way. You may have friends who could benefit from portions of this. Highlight things for them and pass it along! We all are invited.

You are invited!

What kind of an invitation would you want most of all? Fill out the invite specifics:

Who:

What:

Where:

When:

How is this different or similar to God's invitation to you?

What do you consider one of your most **valuable possessions** in the world?

Treasure

1. wealth (such as money, jewels or precious metals) stored up or hoarded.
2. something of great worth or value
3. a collection of precious things

Do you think **prayer** fits the definition of **treasure**? Why or why not?

Collected for You

The best way I know to happiness is prayer. It's the kind of happiness which charges every part of life with grace– a happiness that is full of purpose, which communicates deep peace and makes use of everything. It is a living relationship with God. This book is a resource for that kind of *thriving happiness*.

For decades, I've collected things from hymnals, grad classes, spiritual direction, homilies, books, liturgies, retreats, pilgrimages and most of all, Scripture. So, when my oldest daughter was just about to be Confirmed and I didn't have a gift for her, I decided I would not eat until I had pulled together a readable compilation of resources that have helped me to pray- essentially, giving to her what I consider the best treasure in the world. Three sleepless days later and five pounds lighter, I printed the first copy of this book. Now, years later, that first disheveled piece of love has become a workable handbook for you.

This is my collection of grace. These are the things that keep me on track – help me to thrive. They remind me of who God is and how he found me. The things in this book make it easier for my family to pray together. Sometimes, easier for my husband and me. Knowing that we all exist for each other; I've had you and yours in mind too as I have compiled.

Spiritual resources at times seem hidden and at other times so abundant it is confusing. Here, I have chosen things that are traditional, holy, common and flexible - things that will bring our interior lives into a growing blaze. This is the resource that I have longed for – for myself and for my family, and for you.

This book is meant to open up new treasures for you, to offer you a lifeline when you need it, a Catholic roadmap for clarity and a building block for whatever is next. Perhaps someday you too will compose a collection of grace for yourself and for those you love.

I'd like to read it.

How to Use this Book

I hope this book can be *useful* to you. It is a resource to help you and your family to grow close to God through a deep, educational, personal, consistent and flexible prayer life.

Like a set of tools, it can be used:

- **at random** – providing a few words at a special meal or when you don't know what to do for a time of prayer. I certainly use it in this way.
- **as a reference** – it can help you remember the wording or order for particular prayers like the Rosary or Benediction. Keep it handy to look things up.
- **for your "Go to"** – you can keep it by your kitchen table so that you daily have something to pray in the morning and for meals. Or, keep it by your bedside. For many of us who are concerned by the inundation of technology – even in our prayer lives – this book can free you (and your loved ones) from some of the time you would ordinarily rely on digital help for prayer.
- **like a book in the pew** – so that a family or group has a common starting point – you can all turn to page such and such and it makes it easy for bible study meetings or family prayer.
- **as a coaching tool** – to help a friend or family member connect with Christ and begin to pray regularly.
- **for inspiration** – even if you do not follow this step by step, you can be inspired by how some saints have lived and some of the ways people approach prayer in life.

- **to design** – your own framework. You can let this book guide you to start or edify your own plan of *a consistent life of prayer*. It was ultimately for this reason that I was driven to write this book.

Draw an arrow to the ways **you** are most likely to use this book.

Check the stressors

which you think could be an opportunity for someone to meet Christ in the crisis.

- ☐ Lack of sleep.
- ☐ Chaos in the home.
- ☐ Dating.
- ☐ Loneliness.
- ☐ Divorce.
- ☐ Disconnection from friends/family.
- ☐ Bullying.
- ☐ Expectations.
- ☐ Heavy workload.
- ☐ Guilt.
- ☐ Debt and money.
- ☐ Addictions.
- ☐ Injury or Sickness.
- ☐ Learning disabilities.
- ☐ Sin.
- ☐ Abuse.
- ☐ Confusion.
- ☐ Big responsibilities.
- ☐ Insufficient resources.
- ☐ Other_____

70% of teens report that they feel anxiety and stress are major issues in their community.

Pew Research Center 2019

Not Exactly Thriving

I straightened up from my usual pot scrubbing hunch – dizzy again. My littlest one was still asleep but soon would want to nurse. Ignoring the whirling feeling, I loaded the last few cups in the dishwasher - just a couple more things to get ready before the morning. Maybe I'd have a chance to catch up on emails and pay a few bills. The dizziness passed.

When my doctor heard about my frequent light-headedness, she had ordered a series of tests. After overcoming MRI claustrophobia, filling out forms in all sorts of offices, shelling out money and maxing out my babysitter list, I sat before the last doctor, ready to hear my prognosis. She was a middle-aged ENT. After finding nothing wrong, she calmly said, "You know, stress can do weird things. Do you think that could be your problem?" Oh. Yes. Thank you. That's it.

No scope or blood test could see what another mom could see. Because my problem was, I did not have the capacity to be in ten places at once nor the power to accomplish all my work. And beyond that, there was a deeper problem. In my frenzy, I had put to the side my romance with Christ, exchanging the loving company I kept with God for slavish work. Like a college athlete in exam week, my life was crammed with responsibility. I was trapped with every baseboard I wiped or carpool I organized – over loaded and under-achieving. And yet, soon I was to see that these very same things were part of the path back to the Center of my Life.

But I had become short-fused, intemperate and bitter. My longing for God and inability to respond made me suffer greatly, while the guilt from my ugly behavior compounded daily. In this messy state I attended a lecture about St. Augustine's Confessions. I immersed myself in the compassionate description of the drawn out conversion of poor Augustine and when the speaker reached the pinnacle moment when Augustine let go of sin, hope stirred in me. I hazarded that if this priest could think so insightfully on St. Augustine, perhaps he could help me see a way out of my angst.

This hope did not disappoint. There was a way out. God reached in. I reached out. I re-learned how to pray. I began to see and love God in my mess. I paused a few times each day for solitary consolation with Christ (even if the solitary moment was only in the inner portion of my heart). Through attentiveness to a type of spiritual plan which fit well with my life, I began to grow again. Thriving. In my wonderful chaotic life.

Perhaps you are in a crazy situation yourself. Maybe you used to be close to God but the way your life is now, you cannot see him. You need not move backwards to an ideal place in your past. Nor do you need to worry if you never have been close to God before. God can reach you now. God is in the present. In this state. Here now. In *this* part of your crazy life.

Every person has an experience like this, when you are "not exactly thriving". What is yours?

What does it look like when you are thriving?

List words that describe you when you thrive.

Are you in that place right now?

☐ Yes   ☐ No   ☐ Sort of

Where have you been?

Make a dot on the places in the US that you have visited.

Circle the places you have been globally.

Every place you have ever been, God has been with you.

Anywhere

While our emotions, minds, bodies and relationships cannot thrive at all times, there seems to be good evidence that our souls can – even in a crazy life.

St. Paul says,
"I have learned to be content with whatever I have.
I know what it is to have little, and I know what it is to have plenty.
In any and all circumstances I have learned the secret of being well-fed and of going hungry, of having plenty and of being in need.
I can do all things through him who strengthens me."
Philippians 4:11-13 NRSV

St. Paul had the life and faith to back up this statement (shipwrecked, imprisoned, starvation, exposure). Others too, like St. Philip Neri, St. Bernadette, St. Juan Diego had a powerful joy no matter what. Perhaps joy is not the right word. Faith, peace, energy, security… I struggle to come close to describing what it is that people radiate who have been transformed by God. Even Mother Theresa, who went through deep sorrow of the soul also had this kind of spiritual thriving.

I have been inspired by the story of Fr. Walter Ciszek, S.J. who snuck into Russia as a missionary just before WWII. He was almost immediately arrested as a spy. Even through work camps, solitary confinement and continual threat of death, Fr. Walter was able to experience a deepening of faith. This was, of course completely an act of God. His faith and the closeness he felt was a gift that God gave him.

But the pages of his reflections are full of a desperate urging – compelling his readers that they too can experience intimacy with God through every ordinary and extraordinary circumstance. As I reflect on his writing, it appears to me that at least four things were the vessels of that gift of faith which brought him to thrive.

surrender to God
embrace of circumstances
spiritual plan
generosity to others

1. *A complete and loving intent to surrender to God.* This was whole-hearted even though it was broken and flawed.
2. *An embrace of circumstances – finding God IN them.* Each gritty moment he took as an opportunity to give and receive love with God.
3. *A connection to God through a spiritual plan.* Even through starvation, unending work and torture, he made a morning offering, he recited Mass, he made sacrifices for others, he reflected on Scripture, he did an evening examination of conscience – etc. All throughout his day, he maintained pillars of connection to Christ.
4. *Generous action on behalf of others.* The reason for going to Russia in the first place was to care for those people who were trapped inside the communist walls. He strove to do his difficult forced physical labor and create something helpful for the community which oppressed him. He risked his life many times to hear the confessions of fellow prisoners or to share the Eucharist with a spiritually hungry worker. He was generous with all. In giving his life to God, he gave his life to others.

This same pattern (surrendering, embracing circumstances, faithfully turning to God through the day and living generously) is seen in the lives of many of the saints (probably all of them) helping them to thrive in all sorts of situations. In particular, the Little Flower (St. Thérèse) has led many Christians to reverse cultural norms and rejoice even when life is full of annoyances.

When my youngest daughter was little, I could not go anywhere with her without stopping to pick flowers. She could find them on EVERY trip we took; parking lots, sidewalks and driveways did not deter her. She saw life popping up in the most unusual places and she saw that it was beautiful. I think that is how it is with people of faith. Like the little flowers, they can thrive anywhere.

I want this rock-solid faith. I want to love no matter what and find God everywhere. This is, of course, a gift. I wonder if it is perhaps being offered to me? Or to you? I want this gift for everyone. For my neighbor, for the hungry children in Nigeria, for the day traders at their computers, for the happy grandmother, for my own kids. Perhaps we can open this gift of God. Let us say "yes" with all our intent. Let us find God IN our life. Let us live a life of prayer. Let us be generous. (Let us live prayer.)

Like Father Walter, all of the saints, and little kids like my little daughter, you have powerful thoughts which help you in all sorts of different circumstances. Your thoughts affect how you feel and your feelings affect your actions. What thoughts are driving your success?

thoughts which lead you to thrive...

 personal preferences

It helps to incorporate your own style into the dreams and plans you have for prayer.

In general, when you are thinking about your upcoming events which do you prefer?
(neither is right nor wrong)

☐ Detail plan and structured
☐ Open and spontaneous

What are three steps you took when you succeeded at something difficult? Write them by the path:

a path

Because of your success in other arenas, you already have a sense of how prayer works.

The Work of Cultivation

Prayer is like gardening with God. Just like the parable of the sower and the seed, we can prepare the soil of our hearts so that God's seed takes root. If you are new to an established pattern of prayer, you could consider following a basic plan.

Morning:	Offer up the day (15-90 seconds)
	Read Scripture (1-15 min)
	Reflect/meditate (1-15 min)
Day:	Act of trust / rest / silence (1-30 min)
	Intercede with small sacrifices (1-5 times)
	Aspirations (1 second)
Evening:	Learn from a spiritual book or podcast (1-15 min)
	Examine the day in God's light (1-5 min)

Try adding portions one by one every month or so and figure out what works for your life. The table of contents of this book represents the common elements of a Catholic's life of prayer. You could look through it and with God's wisdom - plan out what would be best for you at this stage. Each day of the week may be different for you. The ways and times we pray will vary greatly by person and by season of life; make it your own. There are so many ways to integrate prayer. Perhaps something very simple. Or, perhaps you work out something extensive.

Recognize that changes happen! What was perfect for you a year ago may not be the spiritual state God has you in now. Be responsive to the work of God within you. Service, conversations or sufferings may take the place of some of these planned devotions. Likewise, you may periodically be given extended time, by God, for dedicated prayer.

You might need lots of flexibility in your plan. Or you may need a friend to help keep you on track and an iron will to persevere. A huge benefit of having a plan is that it helps us to be loyal to God based on our faith, not on our momentary feelings. But our attentiveness to a plan should never become a loveless routine! It is meant to foster connection – and support thriving in your circumstances.

Alternatively, some people's prayer plans look like this:

Daily:	15 minutes of quiet prayer Rosary Read a spiritual book Mass/Communion Service (when I can)
Weekly:	Sunday Mass Bible study Volunteer Soup kitchen Reach out to friends
Monthly:	Sacrament of Reconciliation Recollection (~3 hours of silence)
Yearly:	Retreat

Not every season has to have an intricate plan. One year of my life, I laid out my plan for prayer very simply. I told God,

> *"My life is so unstable right now.*
> *All I can do is trust you.*
> *Every day I will look to your Holy Spirit*
> *to see what I should do."*

It was a fantastic year, filled with prayer, service and light. So, as you make a plan, do so with ease and freedom. This is not a homework assignment that needs to be turned in- it is a feast to enjoy. You are not under obligation. Don't let guilt creep up on you because there is much you are not doing or because you couldn't get to ¾ of your plan. No worries. Ultimately, the only thing we need to do is follow God, enjoy Mass on Sunday and live in love.

On the flip side, recognize that you have a right to prayer and time with your Lord (even if it takes daily miracles to find those moments). You are not a slave to your life. You have been freed by Christ to live in the Spirit.

The garden of grace is open to you!

your right to pray

Life can feel like a battle at times. There are so many demands on us all. Your right to pray is in a warzone that gets tested the most.

However, you have a God-given right to spend time daily with the creator of the heavens and the earth – and you. What will you do with this right?

In order to answer that question, look at the path you made on page 8. How can you incorporate your ideas into pursuing your right to pray?

List some of the **people** who have **helped you** to be close **to God**.

Write their names in the frames.

Who are you **helping**?

Write a prayer for them now.

Helping Others in Prayer

Many parents and grandparents want to teach their good families to pray, but they flounder at times with what to do. Or, friends want to help each other along but find it hard to cross over into action. This book is meant to aid in helping someone to pray.

If you live with the person you are trying to encourage, keep this book in a handy place so you can use it as key moments arise. For me, that's near the kitchen. I use it to make recommendations for what my kids could read while eating breakfast or pick a scripture verse to memorize together. You can use it to help them find a little time during the day to connect with God. Or, consider giving a copy of this book to each person in the family so that you can pray together in the morning, at bedtime, or on Sunday nights.

If you are helping along a friend or relative who lives farther away, you can exc hange favorite prayers, talk about your own prayer goals and use the book to pray together. My best friend and I live 1000 miles apart and yet we pray together on the phone a couple times each month.

We lear n best by doing. So, when helping a loved one along, use this book to move from discussion into honest prayer. When I first wrote this book for my daughter, I gave it to her hoping it would bring her a rich path for prayer. Instead, it sat on her nightstand collecting dust. This is because the faith is not passed on through a book alone. It is through *accompanying* our loved ones that they learn to live in prayer. When my spiritual life is transparent and welcoming, my children learn the faith. Catholic resources get used when I use them *with* my kids. (And yes, my oldest daughter prays beautifully).

Leading others into an active relationship with God is extremely hard and sensitive work. However, it might be the most important thing you will ever do. Keep on.

My *Flexible* Plan

As you start out, write down some of your own hopes for prayer. You can make an initial plan and then revisit it to make it more appropriate to your life. Scan through the book and see which chapters most attract you. Then, complete the prayer to the right.

- ❑ What are your general hopes for prayer?

- ❑ How do you want to achieve that?

- ❑ Daily plan:

- ❑ Chapters which may help:

- ❑ Other ideas:

Dear God, I believe that you are...

My own preferences and personality are important to you. I want to a make a life of prayer which looks like...

I have a choice in this relationship and I chose to...

Prayer is something people learn to do. Specifically, I want to thrive...

Love,

Chapter 1

Intending the Best

Junior year in high school, while studying the founding of our nation, my big-mustached history teacher glared through his coke bottle lens glasses and provoked us, "What are you living for? What is the purpose of life?" The class fidgeted. "Umm, to be happy?" "To make a million dollars." "To be successful."

The question resounded with me. My own heart had been asking it with every volleyball game we won, every "A" paper I got, every date I went on. Because my success, my teenage triumphs, were not actually making me happy. But of course, I longed to be so. "Yeah, to be happy. That's what I'm living for," I begrudgingly agreed.

We had played right into our masterful teacher's hands. Turns out our ideas were completely contrary from what motivated the pilgrims. They, he said, lived to give glory to God. Immediately it sounded right. That's what I want. Yes, that is what I'm made for. That's what I'll do.

I had been Catholic all my life. I had been loving, praying and living for God in many ordinary ways that all Christians do. But now it came to the forefront of my mind. I chose it. I intended it. And when I did, I stopped looking for happiness and started to serve. But happiness found me as I served the Glorious God. And what felt like my intention, quickly revealed itself to be the powerful work of a God who was pursuing me. Mysteriously disrobing his eternal intentions for me through every external circumstance and internal burning.

I hope that as you read this chapter, you can examine your own purpose for living. Your hopes, your deepest and best intentions. What intentions would you like to awaken? Explicitly bring them to mind and you may discover, as I did, that God is already active within you – whispering from within, his own intentions for you.

What do you want with all your heart?

What do you live for?

Did you catch that?

Look at this passage again. Why did God create man*? Underline that part.

Give one juicy word to describe God's tone as conveyed by this passage.

What does it feel like *on the inside* to be urged on by the love of Christ?

What does it look like *on the outside*?

*man In this instance, "man" is not talking about gender, it refers to every single human that ever lived.

Purpose

In this section you can begin by clarifying your own purpose in life, your intentions to live close to God and to allow him to animate your life. Allow the readings and prayers here to help you to do so. Come back to them frequently to live in these goals.

Prologue to the Catechism of the Catholic Church
A prologue sets the tone for the whole book. Here, we see that the tone of the most popular "instruction manual" of the church is one of invitation.

I. The life of man - to know and love God

1 God, infinitely perfect and blessed in himself, in a plan of sheer goodness freely created man to make him share in his own blessed life. For this reason, at every time and in every place, God draws close to man. He calls man to seek him, to know him, to love him with all his strength. He calls together all men, scattered and divided by sin, into the unity of his family, the Church. To accomplish this, when the fullness of time had come, God sent his Son as Redeemer and Saviour. In his Son and through him, he invites men to become, in the Holy Spirit, his adopted children and thus heirs of his blessed life….

3 Those who with God's help have welcomed Christ's call and freely responded to it are urged on by love of Christ to proclaim the Good News everywhere in the world. This treasure, received from the apostles, has been faithfully guarded by their successors. All Christ's faithful are called to hand it on from generation to generation, by professing the faith, by living it in fraternal sharing, and by celebrating it in liturgy and prayer.

The First Principle and Foundation

This prayer is the starting point of the Spiritual Exercises of St. Ignatius of Loyola. This might be my all-time favorite passage for rooting my outlook on life in the truth.

The goal of our life is to live with God forever.
God, who loves us, gave us life.
Our own response of love allows God's life
to flow into us without limit.

All the things in this world are gifts from God,
presented to us so that we can know God more easily
and make a return of love more readily.
As a result, we appreciate and use all these gifts of God
insofar as they help us to develop as loving persons.
But if any of these gifts become the center of our lives,
they displace God and so hinder our growth toward our goal.

In everyday life, then, we must hold ourselves in balance
before all of these created gifts insofar as we have a choice
and are not bound by some obligation.
We should not fix our desires on health or sickness,
wealth or poverty, success or failure, a long life or a short one,
for everything has the potential of calling forth in us
a deeper response to our life in God.

Our only desire and our one choice should be this:
I want and I choose what better leads
to God's deepening his life in me.

List 3 things in your life that you usually hold in a good balance –

How do you know when something in your life is off balance?

What are two things you need help balancing? Say a brief prayer about it, asking for help.

It feels good when God is at the center.

memorize

Until the later part of the 20th century, people used to memorize catechism questions and answers word for word. They did this so that the teachings of the church and reasons for faith were rooted in their minds.

Which of these questions and answers would you find most helpful to memorize – to store and etch into your mind? Rewrite it here:

Collection of Grace

Baltimore Catechism

The Baltimore Catechism schooled many of our beloved baby boomers in the ways of the Church. While it fell out of common use, this nugget has always helped me.

The Purpose of Man's Existence-
Lesson 1
from the Baltimore Catechism

1. *Who made us?*
God made us.

In the beginning, God created heaven and earth. (Genesis 1:1)

2. *Who is God?*
God is the Supreme Being, infinitely perfect, who made all things and keeps them in existence.

In him we live and move and have our being. (Acts 17:28)

3. *Why did God make us?*
God made us to show forth His goodness and to share with us His everlasting happiness in heaven.

Eye has not seen nor ear heard, nor has it entered into the heart of man, what things God has prepared for those who love him. (I Corinthians 2:9)

And from B. Catechism 1:
God made me to know Him, to love Him, and to serve Him in this world, and to be happy with Him forever in heaven.

4. *What must we do to gain the happiness of heaven?*
To gain the happiness of heaven we must know, love, and serve God in this world.

Lay not up to yourselves treasures on earth; where the rust and moth consume and where thieves break through and steal. But lay up to yourselves treasures in heaven; where neither the rust nor moth doth consume, and where thieves do not break through nor steal. (Matthew 6:19-20)

5. *From whom do we learn to know, love, and serve God?*
We learn to know, love, and serve God from Jesus Christ, the Son of God, who teaches us through the Catholic Church.

I have come a light into the world that whoever believes in Me may not remain in darkness. (John 12:46)

6. *Where do we find the chief truths taught by Jesus Christ through the Catholic Church?*
We find the chief truths taught by Jesus Christ through the Catholic Church in the Apostles' Creed.

Basics of the Faith

These concepts are foundational to a Christian's understanding of who God is and what he asks of us. Perhaps they can be a source of grounding and inspiration for you as you think through your purpose and intentions for life.

At the Heart of it All

This is the starting point of everything and the thought to which we always need to return.

God is with you.
You are loved.

Sh'ma Israel

In Mark's Gospel, when Jesus was asked about the most important commandment, he quoted this ancient prayer from Deuteronomy.

Hear, O Israel!
The Lord our God is Lord alone!
You shall love the Lord your God
with all your heart,
with all your soul,
with all your mind,
and with all your strength.

The second is this: "You shall love your neighbor as yourself."
There is no other commandment greater than these.

Very familiar?

Have you heard these things many times before? Sometimes we cannot notice the power of concepts we hear so often. At other times the familiar becomes part of ourselves and beloved without us really knowing a lot about it- integrated but unexplored.

What about you? On a scale of 1-5, how new, explored, powerful or integrated are the page 17 concepts to you?

New
1   2   3   4   5

Explored
1   2   3   4   5

Powerful
1   2   3   4   5

Integrated
1   2   3   4   5

The words matter

Define 5 words from the Nicene Creed that a kid would have a hard time understanding. Look up the meanings if you need.

_____ :

_____ :

_____ :

_____ :

_____ :

The Nicene Creed

This creed clarified our beliefs in Jesus at the council of Nicea in 325. This profession is held in common with Catholics, all Eastern churches and most Protestant churches.

I believe in one God, the Father almighty,
maker of heaven and earth,
of all things visible and invisible.

I believe in one Lord Jesus Christ,
the Only Begotten Son of God,
born of the Father before all ages.
God from God, Light from Light,
true God from true God,
begotten, not made, consubstantial with the Father;
through him all things were made.

For us men and for our salvation
he came down from heaven,
and by the Holy Spirit was incarnate of the Virgin Mary,
and became man.

For our sake he was crucified under Pontius Pilate,
he suffered death and was buried,
and rose again on the third day
in accordance with the Scriptures.

He ascended into heaven
and is seated at the right hand of the Father.
He will come again in glory
to judge the living and the dead
and his kingdom will have no end.

I believe in the Holy Spirit, the Lord, the giver of life,
who proceeds from the Father and the Son,
who with the Father and the Son is adored and glorified,
who has spoken through the prophets.

I believe in one, holy, catholic and apostolic Church.
I confess one Baptism for the forgiveness of sins
and I look forward to the resurrection of the dead
and the life of the world to come.

Summary of the Gospel

It is good to be clear about the heart of the Good News. There is nothing official about this summary; it is an adaption of the Crux bible study from Fellowship of Catholic University Students.

1. We are made good in God's image, made for relationship.
2. We became broken through sin.
3. Jesus, truly God and truly human, comes to us to bring us back.
4. Jesus taught about the kingdom of God through miracles, healings, stories and conversations.
5. Through the grace of Jesus giving his life on the cross for us and rising from the dead, God heals our brokenness.
6. God, our generous Father, eagerly forgives and invites us to reside with him as sons and daughters.
7. We respond.
8. Empowered by the Spirit, we live with God in the Church through the Apostles' teaching, community, the breaking of the bread and prayer.

Even Shorter Gospel Summary

1. Made for relationship
2. Broken through sin
3. God becomes one of us
4. Jesus shows us the way
5. His death and resurrection heal us
6. God invites us back
7. We respond
8. We live in the Church

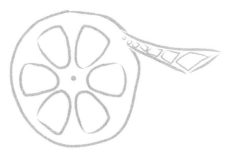

Go through each of the points in the summary and visualize it – as if a movie was playing in your head. What do you notice?

See it in your mind

It takes the right space to really be able to pray. Most often times, this "space" is created on the inside of a person. Read through this prayer and describe the internal and external space that would be needed for you to pray this with honesty and meaning.

External space:

Internal space:

We need space to pray honestly.

Response to the Gospel

Responding to the Good News is necessary to experience its grace. You did this if and when you were baptized. St. Teresa of Avila gave her life to God 50 times a day. Likewise, you have responded to the Gospel every time you crossed yourself with Holy Water, every time you cared for someone out of compassion and every time you have gone to church. Still, if you have never intentionally and mindfully decided to follow Christ, perhaps now is a good time. Reaffirm this often.

I believe, God, my Father, that you love me
and that you sent your son, Jesus,
to take on my flesh and my experience.

I admit that I have sinned and turned away from you.
Please forgive me.

Thank you, Jesus, for dying on the cross and taking every sin, problem and burden of mine upon yourself.

I believe that you rose from the dead
and that you have conquered my own sin and death.
Thank you for bringing me to new life.

I entrust myself completely to you.
Every part of me and my life
is open.

Holy Spirit, please come reign in me
and transform me into the person whom the Father has made me to be.

Let me live and serve in communion with your family, the Church, and give my life to your mission of love.

My *Flexible* Plan

Write down your own intentions. Get clear about your commitments. With pen in hand, you can surrender to God and orient your life to him.

What do I intend with my life?

❑ My life commitment to God:

❑ Overall purpose:

❑ Things that are always important to me:

❑ Characteristics I want to carry:

Dear God, the purpose you created me for is …

At this point, I mostly want…

I commit myself to you by…

Please help my trust …

Love,

Chapter 2

Connecting Throughout the Day

My sister is a nun. Well, technically she is a "sister", not a nun. A nun is someone who remains always cloistered in a convent. But everyone calls sisters, "nuns" so I do too. The first time I visited her convent, I was struck by the feeling of holiness that pervaded every little thing. It seemed that they turned 100 mundane actions into reminders of their spiritual life. Every time they pass the chapel, they genuflect. They kiss their scapulars (part of their clothing which reminds them of Mary's protection) whenever they put on an apron (or something like that); they keep their veils ship-shape (which reminds them that they are brides of Christ). Even wearing shoes is an act of faith – it reminds them to have "feet fitted for the readiness of spreading the Gospel." And bells! Always beautiful bells calling the sisters to make a visit to the chapel for a communal prayer. Morning, day, evening, night. Always a prayer for this or that moment. Visually too, their home speaks of Christ. Their walls hold either a simple crucifix or a stirringly spiritual painting.

When I returned home from my visit, I began to notice the many things in my own life that called out for opportunities to turn to God in the midst of my day. The newness of morning, my lunch, driving, that church I just passed, those chores again, the sound of an ambulance, the fatigue of evening- all of it can be a trigger to open ourselves again to the God who charges all of life with his own love.

God is always with you! Therefore, you can be united even in the midst of a busy workday. Here you will find help to establish connection for each moment. Not only can you experience abiding peace but also you can enjoy doing his will – living your life through his power and not only your own.

The prayers in this section are about connecting with God. It is meant to give you lots of ideas and options but nothing in here is meant to be a formula for the only right way. All of these things arose from people's relationships with God. Lean on the things that attract you, let go of what does not jive.

Your relationship counts

The depth and connection of your relationship depends upon you and God.

How do you usually feel in the morning? Why?

God is interested and loves YOU- the you that you are today, were yesterday and will be tomorrow.

Incorporating your own personality and circumstances, how can you bring yourself to God and invite him into the very beginning of your day?

Morning Offerings

A morning offering is a little prayer that you say within the first few moments of getting up. Basically, you are dedicating your life to God at the start of each day. A song, a psalm, a written prayer or a spontaneous conversation can be a morning offering.

Morning Offering

This is one of the most common traditional morning offerings.

O Jesus,
through the Immaculate Heart of Mary,
I offer You my prayers, works,
joys and sufferings
of this day for all the intentions
of Your Sacred Heart,
in union with the Holy Sacrifice of the Mass
throughout the world,
in reparation for my sins,
for the intentions of all my relatives and friends,
and in particular
for the intentions of the Holy Father.

Invitatory

These phrases are said first thing in the morning by monks, nuns, sisters, priests and lay people all around the world who are praying the "invitatory" or "morning prayer" of the Liturgy of the Hours.

| Leader: | Lord, open my lips |
| All: | and my mouth will declare your praise. |

| Leader: | O God, come to my assistance. |
| All: | O Lord, make haste to help me. |

7Little Child's Morning Offering

Sometimes it is good to keep things simple.

Good morning, Jesus.
I love you.
I will follow you today.

Prayer for Today
Good Morning, Jesus! I love you. I praise you.
Let us be together this day in everything I do,
every place I go and in every person I see.
Please help me with the things that will be difficult.
I will remember your love for me on the cross.
And in all the things that are joyful today,
it will be for you!

Morning Offering to Begin this Day
In the name of our Lord Jesus Christ I will begin this day.
I thank you, Lord, for having preserved me during the night.
I will do my best to make all I do today pleasing to You and in accordance with Your will.
My dear mother Mary, watch over me this day.
My Guardian Angel, take care of me.
St. Joseph and all you saints of God, pray for me...

A Morning Prayer by St. Thérèse
O my God! I offer Thee all my actions of this day for the intentions and for the glory of the Sacred Heart of Jesus. I desire to sanctify every beat of my heart, my every thought, my simplest works, by uniting them to His infinite merits; and I wish to make reparation for my sins by casting them into the furnace of His Merciful Love.

O my God! I ask of Thee for myself and for those whom I hold dear, the grace to fulfill perfectly Thy Holy Will, to accept for love of Thee the joys and sorrows of this passing life, so that we may one day be united together in heaven for all Eternity.

God's mercy is new every morning.

All of heaven on your side.

Imagine that when you wake up in the morning, you could see all of heaven cheering you on. Draw what you see or find a picture online.

Collection of Grace

Carrie's Morning Prayer

My dear Lord Jesus, thank you for this day and for my life! I love you. Always you have been with me and I praise you in the depth of my heart where you reside.

Casting myself into the Father's loving hands, I place my joyful faith. O Jesus, my comfort, my peace and my love, it is you whom I desire in all that I am, all that I do, all that I think, feel and will. With the fellowship of your Holy Spirit, I will accept what comes this day as a gift from you and to you. Thank you, thank you, for the treasures you have given me. Let it all be for you.

Jesus, I trust you. You know all that this day holds and you will be with me in everything. I give myself – all of me and mine firmly into your hands.

Without you I can do nothing and with you I can do the Father's will. For what shall I ask this day? … For my family. For all whom I know and love. For the grace to live this day well- to seek you in everything, to commune with you continually, to be joyfully trusting, to see you in my family and to turn to you in my need.

With your own passion, I say "YES" this day.

Sign Language Morning Offering

Young children love to sign the italicized words. You can look up the motions for this at www.handspeak.com

I give myself to your *beautiful* love.
I want to be *good* with your strength from above.

Your *cross* will guide all I do and *say*.
Lord Jesus Christ, please *hold my hand* today.

Morning Exclamation

One of my mom's favorite thoughts first thing in the morning:

This is the day the Lord has made, let us rejoice and be glad in it! Psalm 118:24

Canticle of Zechariah

By reciting this canticle from Luke 1:68-79, you will be joining the prayers of millions of religious around the world who are saying morning prayer.

Blessed be the Lord, the God of Israel;
he has come to his people and set them free.

He has raised up for us a mighty savior,
born of the house of his servant David.

Through his holy prophets he promised of old
that he would save us from our enemies,
from the hands of all who hate us.

He promised to show mercy to our fathers
and to remember his holy covenant.

This was the oath he swore to our father Abraham:
to set us free from the hands of our enemies,
free to worship him without fear,
holy and righteous in his sight all the days of our life.

You, my child, shall be called the prophet of the Most High;
for you will go before the Lord to prepare his way,
to give his people knowledge of salvation
by the forgiveness of their sins.

In the tender compassion of our God
the dawn from on high shall break upon us,
to shine on those who dwell in darkness and
the shadow of death,
and to guide our feet into the way of peace.

Read all of the morning offerings.

Find a phrase of **prayerful action** which is most curious to you.

Highlight or underline it and explain why you chose that one.

Using the formula in the box on the bottom write of this page,

compose your own morning offering:

Morning Prayer

Find a few other prayers that are perfect for the morning in the section on Praise. There are a handful of psalms that are repeated often in the liturgy of the hours.

Prayer to Begin Work

This is an important prayer, not only at the start of the day but before beginning any significant action.

Direct, we beseech you, O Lord,
our actions by your holy inspirations,
and carry them on
by your gracious assistance,
that every prayer and work of ours
may begin always with you,
and through you come to completion.

Or a different translation:

Lord, may everything we do
Begin with your inspiration
And continue with your help
So that all our prayers and works
May begin in you
And by you be happily ended.

From the Heart – In the Morning

It is likely that your own spontaneous thoughts and conversation with God are unpretentious and Spirit led first thing in the morning. While not wanting to stifle your natural impulses, here's a bit of a formula to get you going. Make the morning offering your own.

1. Thank God.
2. Offer everything from the upcoming day to Him.
3. Ask for his presence / guidance or help.
4. Unite yourself with Jesus and the Church.

Continual Prayer

These are prayers and practices which can help you to continually be aware of God in your midst and to unite yourself to him throughout the whole day. These turn mundane life into prayer.

The Practice of the Presence of God

The Carmelite Brother Lawrence wrote in the 17th century about being with God at the center of every moment. These quotes can help us to continually live in a simple but profound communion with God – which is the heart of prayer.

"His prayer was nothing else but a sense of the presence of God, his soul being at that time insensible to everything but Divine love: and that when the appointed times of prayer were past, he found no difference, because he still continued with God, praising and blessing Him with all his might, so that he passed his life in continual joy."

"We must know before we can love. In order to know God, we must often think of Him; and when we come to love Him, we shall then also think of Him often, for our heart will be with our treasure."

"He does not ask much of us, merely a thought of Him from time to time, a little act of adoration, sometimes to ask for His grace, sometimes to offer Him your sufferings, at other times to thank Him for the graces, past and present, He has bestowed on you, in the midst of your troubles to take solace in Him as often as you can. Lift up your heart to Him during your meals and in company; the least little remembrance will always be the most pleasing to Him. One need not cry out very loudly; He is nearer to us than we think."

"For my part I keep myself retired with Him in the depth of the center of my soul as much as I can; and while I am so with Him I fear nothing."

"with Him in the depth of my center"

When you stub your toe, you immediately notice it. If you try, you can pay attention to any part of you- your shoulder, around your waistband, your chin… but what about the depth of your center? Where is the depth of your center? How can you notice God there?

Draw an arrow to the **aspiration or whisper** that you would like to try this week.

And/or write your own:

Aspirations

An aspiration is a prayer that you say with your breath, repeated all day long. Some people choose or create an aspiration that will help them during a particular day, week or season of life. Whenever you waiver or are troubled even a bit, you can say the prayer. A scripture verse would also make a great aspiration. Here are a few traditional aspirations for you to consider:

Come, Holy Spirit.
Lord Jesus, Son of the Living God, have mercy on me, a sinner.
Jesus, have mercy.
Blessed be God!
Heart of Jesus, I put my trust in Thee!
Jesus, I trust in You!
Jesus, my God, I love Thee above all things!
Jesus, Son of David, have mercy on me!
My God and my all.
Praised be Jesus Christ, now and forevermore.

Affectionate Whispers

You can speak to God all day long, whispering little things like this to him – like a love note you are sending.

I love you.
Thank you!
You are good.
You make me happy.
I need you.
You are everything to me.
I trust you.

Making Sacrifices

We Christians, (little Christs) are called to share in the sufferings of Jesus. And in willingly accepting hardship and making sacrifices, we join our lives to his holy sacrifice on the cross. In doing so, we draw closer to him and are effectual in helping others around the world and in the body of Christ. Here are some active sacrifices for you to consider.

- Smile even when you are grumpy
- Skip a boastful outburst you were going to say
- Be extra kind
- Let another person win an insignificant banter
- Sleep on the floor or without a pillow
- Fast from part of your meal
- Use good posture
- Keep a family member company during your leisure time
- Observe another and do something to make her happy
- Obey the speed limit and rules of the road
- Volunteer service hours
- Make good eye contact
- Listen reflectively
- Vie for someone else's favorites instead of your own
- Offer up your sacrifices for specific people or general concerns

Interior Senses to Mortify

All three of these senses are good, God given gifts. Frequently making a tiny act to offer them to God can help us to enjoy and use the gifts in the way God intends for us- rather than getting led by what is lower.

Memory (the past)
"Jesus, I give you my memory…"

Curiosity (the present)
"Jesus, I give you my curiosity…"

Imagination (the future)
"Jesus, I give you my imagination…"

the reason
for sacrifice and mortification is...

interior freedom & ability to love

Mortify
2: to subdue or deaden (bodily appetites, etc.) especially by abstinence

How could mortifying interior senses or making a sacrifice lead to freedom or the ability to love?

On this page or the previous, highlight a small sacrifice or mortification you will try this week. Or write your own:

For the sake of...

As you make this sacrifice/mortification this week, who would you like to pray for? Write the name of the person or intention here:

Collection of Grace

Unite Our Actions with Christ

All of the good things we do – especially our duties, become prayer when we unite ourselves with Christ. Here are everyday things that become prayer when we do them with excellence and love.

Jesus, I unite myself to you as I ...
- Do chores and errands
- Act with kindness to siblings
- Honor my parents
- Tend to the things in my state of life (homework, bills, play)
- Act as a good friend
- Maintain fitness and health

Common Mortifications

Small daily acts of mortification (dying to yourself) enable you to exercise self-control which will help when you are tested in larger situations. Consider making a very tiny sacrifice in each one of these categories every day.

Speech
ex: I will skip the story I wanted to tell and instead, listen.

Sight
ex: I will not look at that beautiful field as I pass by so that someday if I am tempted elsewhere, I will have the power to look away.

Food
ex: I will eat all of the pickle that I do not like.

Leisure
ex: I will play a board game with my brother for 20 minutes instead of reading my book.

Comfort
ex: For this evening, I will put on a light sweater instead my big sweatshirt.

Specific Activity Prayers

We turn to God frequently. We trust.

Meeting with Friends
Thank you, God, for friendship. Please give me goodness as I interact.

Studying or Taking a Test
May I give you glory through my studies. Help me to remember and perceive well. Fix me firmly to the Truth.

Using Screens
I commit to use technology only for your purposes. Thanks for this tool. Protect me from overuse and help me to be happily productive.

Household Chores
Thank you for the humility of concrete work. Help me to find and serve you, Jesus, in the most menial tasks.

Homework
Jesus, please help me to learn and be efficient. I dedicate this time to you.

Writing Emails or Texts
Please, may I say your words.

Driving
Holy Spirit, please guide me along the way. Keep me alert and wise. Please protect me and those on my path.

During a Challenge
Draw your strength from the Lord and from his mighty power. 11 Put on the armor of God so that you may be able to stand firm against the tactics of the devil. 12 For our struggle is not with flesh and blood but with the principalities, with the powers, with the world rulers of this present darkness, with the evil spirits in the heavens. 13 Therefore, put on the armor of God, that you may be able to resist on the evil day and, having done everything, to hold your ground. 14 So stand fast with your loins girded in truth, clothed with righteousness as a breastplate, 15 and your feet shod in readiness for the gospel of peace. 16 In all circumstances, hold faith as a shield, to quench all [the] flaming arrows of the evil one. 17 And take the helmet of salvation and the sword of the Spirit, which is the word of God. – Ephesians 6:10-17

What activity in your day could really benefit from having a **quick prayer** said right before starting?

Just for fun

Food preferences. What is yours?

- ❏ Fruit all day every day
- ❏ Burger and fries
- ❏ Grandma's pasta
- ❏ Fish – fresh or grilled
- ❏ Cereal straight from the box
- ❏ Sweets!!!!!
- ❏ Nothing ever appeals.
- ❏ I am happy to eat anything.
- ❏ Other::_____

How does prayer before meals effect the connection of the **community around the table?**

Mealtime Prayers

Since mealtime is frequent, sustaining and communal, it is a perfect moment to pause for prayer.

Bless Us, O Lord
Bless us, O Lord,
and these thy gifts
which we are about to receive
from thy bounty
through Christ, Our Lord.

Grateful Hearts
Give us grateful hearts,
O Father,
for all your kindness,
and make us mindful
of the needs of others.

About to Receive
For this
and all we are about to receive,
make us truly grateful, Lord.
Through Christ, we pray.

So Many
In a world
where so many are hungry,
May we eat this food
with humble hearts;
In a world where so many are lonely,
May we share this fellowship
with joy.

In Fellowship
Lord, Our God,
you are the giver
of all that is good.

In fellowship with each other
and your people everywhere,
we thank you for your love.

Please, bless this mealtime,
and those all around the world,
that we may enjoy you
and do well in all our actions.

Be Present
Be present at our table, Lord!
Be here
and everywhere adored.
Your mercies bless,
and grant that we
May strengthened
for thy service be.

From Your Hand
From your hand
comes every good,
We thank you
for our daily food.
And with it Lord,
your blessing give,
And to your glory
may we live.

34

All His Good Gifts
Blessed be God, eternal king,
for these and all his good gifts to us.

Good Food and Friends
For good food and those who prepare it,
for good friends with whom to share it,
we thank you, Lord.

Be Our Guest
Come, Lord Jesus, be our guest,
and let these gifts to us be blessed.

Your words

Using the formula in the box
(or your own way), write your own

prayer for a meal time

Include the things that are
important to YOU.

From the Heart – at Mealtime
Many people get nervous about praying out loud. Here's a simple formula that you can apply to mealtime or anytime people are gathered together.

✝ Make the sign of the cross.
1. Say thank you to God. Think of something that *relates to why all of you are gathered* on that occasion.
2. Ask for God's help. Connect it again to *something that is related to what your group is doing* or what you all are focused on. You can pray for yourselves or for others around the world.
3. Say Amen.
✝ Make the sign of the cross.

Here's a quick summary:

Thank you, God, for _____.
Please, _____.
Amen

Remember to talk to God (not to the people around you). However, everyone present counts because you are speaking on their behalf.

Do you have a drawer or box that is filled with random things? It can be fun to open it up and pick up this object or that nick-knack. Some of the things are beautiful little treasures, others useful mundane things, and some of it is just plain junk that you may wonder why you kept. Looking through your day is kind of like rummaging through a box like that.

Some people like to go chronologically – they think about the early morning and view the blessings and the struggles from that time period- then move to mid-morning/lunch time, and do the same, etc. Others look first for all the things they are grateful for from the whole day and then move on to their all their struggles. You do not have to work super hard to see the day in any "right" or "wrong" way – just let the ideas and images come to you.

Have a look

Take 1-5 minutes and try this prayer now, looking at this day.

Evening / Bedtime

Praying at bedtime seems to be universal. Keep going with the good things you do! Here are some other ideas to try. Remember that many other prayers from this book would be great at bedtime as well.

Prayerful Review of the Day / Examen

St. Ignatius recommended that at the end of every day Christians reflect on the past 24 hours. He said that if we do no other prayer during the day, at least do this one. There are many variations of this Jesuit prayer.

<u>Pray for Light</u>
Ask that you can look at this day through God's eyes.
"Holy Spirit, please enlighten my mind so I may see this past day with truth and love."

<u>Gratitude</u>
Recall the moments for which you are most thankful (the blessings, gifts, high points, presence of God). Converse with Jesus and listen to what these good things mean.
"Thank you... Jesus, you are... This is special because..."
"I offer this back to you with love."

<u>Struggle</u>
From this day, for what am I least thankful? Find the small or big moments of disappointment, sin, hurt, failure – from others or from yourself. Converse with Jesus and listen to what needs healing.
"Please forgive me... I'm sad... Please help..."
"I offer this back to you with love."

<u>Tomorrow with Christ</u>
Ask and receive what you need for tomorrow.
"What help, concept, resolution or peace shall I carry in my heart for tomorrow? I end with love and hope."

Magnificat

When Mary, the Mother of God, became filled with the Holy Spirit, she prayed this song, recorded in Lk 1:46-55. It is prayed every day in the evening, at Vespers.

My soul proclaims the greatness of the Lord,
my spirit rejoices in God my Savior
for he has looked with favor on his lowly servant.
From this day all generations will call me blessed:
the Almighty has done great things for me,
and holy is his Name.

He has mercy on those who fear him
in every generation.
He has shown the strength of his arm,
he has scattered the proud in their conceit.

He has cast down the mighty from their thrones,
and has lifted up the lowly.
He has filled the hungry with good things,
and the rich he has sent away empty.

He has come to the help of his servant Israel
for he remembered his promise of mercy,
the promise he made to our fathers,
to Abraham and his children forever.

Now I Lay me Down to Sleep

Many little children learn this prayer.

Now I lay me down to sleep,
I pray the Lord my soul to keep.
May angels watch me through the night.
And keep me in their blessed sight.

And a portion my parents added:
Please bless Mommy and Daddy,
my siblings and all my friends and relatives
and help me to be good.

Sleep habits

Sometimes prayer is like sleep – a restorative, trusting, surrender, which feels peaceful and comforting, equipping us to serve and live another day with joy. But many of us do not get this kind of sleep regularly. What about you?

Mark the line indicating how much you agree with the statement.

I sleep about 8-9 hours
yes ----------------------------------no

I fall asleep within about 20 min
yes ----------------------------------no

Things I do before bed (routine) are healthy/helpful to sleep.
yes ----------------------------------no

It is dark in my room
yes ----------------------------------no

My room is free of electronics
yes ----------------------------------no

What changes could you make to become more restful during the night? Write about them.

Journal B4 bed

Many people journal before going to bed. Try it here, writing to God about your day.

Collection of Grace

Byzantine Night Prayer (abbreviated)

I was introduced to this solemn prayer by watching Matt Fradd's family pray together. They chanted this - even in their own home! Notice how the rhythm of the prayer mounds upon itself.

In the Name of the Father and of the Son and of the Holy Spirit. Amen.

Glory to You, our God, Glory to You!

O Heavenly King,
the Comforter; the Spirit of Truth, Who are in all places and fill all things; Treasurer of blessings and Giver of life, come and dwell within us and cleanse us from every blemish and save our souls,
O blessed One.

Holy God, Holy Mighty One, Holy Immortal One,
have mercy on us. (3xs)

Glory to the Father and to the Son and to the Holy Spirit, now and ever and forever. Amen.

O Most Holy Trinity, have mercy on us; O Lord, cleanse us of our sins; O Master, forgive our transgressions; O Holy One, come to us and heal our infirmities for Your Name's sake.

Lord, have mercy. (3xs)

Glory to the Father ...
Our Father (Lord's Prayer)

Lord Have Mercy. (12xs)

Glory to the Father ...

Come, let us adore God, our King.

Come, let us adore Christ, our King and our God.

Come, let us adore and bow down to Christ Himself, our King and our God.

The day is now over, Lord: I thank You. Let this evening and this night pass without sin, O Saviour, and save me.

Glory to the Father and to the Son and to the Holy Spirit:

Now that the day is over, Master: I glorify You and ask that this evening and night be without sin. Now and ever and forever. Amen

Now that the day has run its course, Holy One: I praise You and ask that this evening and night may be without sin; grant this, O Saviour and save me!

Psalm 4

Psalm 4 can be prayed to offer the craziness of life into God's hands at the close of the day.

Answer me when I call, my saving God.
   When troubles hem me in, set me free;
   take pity on me, hear my prayer.
How long, O people, will you be hard of heart?
   Why do you love what is worthless, chase after lies?
Know that the Lord works wonders for his faithful one;
   the Lord hears when I call out to him.
Tremble and sin no more;
   weep bitterly within your hearts,
   wail upon your beds,
Offer fitting sacrifices
   and trust in the Lord.
Many say, "May we see better times!
   Lord, show us the light of your face!"
But you have given my heart more joy
   than they have when grain and wine abound.
In peace I will lie down and fall asleep,
   for you alone, Lord, make me secure.

Penitential Act

Want to rest in peace? Toss all your sins from the day to the Lord and ask his forgiveness. You can use this penitential prayer from Mass or any other from you heart. Monks, priests, nuns and sisters all say some kind of penitential act before they go to bed.

724443I confess to almighty God
and to you, my brothers and sisters,
that I have greatly sinned,
in my thoughts and in my words,
in what I have done and in what I have failed to do,

through my fault, through my fault,
through my most grievous fault;
therefore, I ask blessed Mary ever-Virgin,
all the Angels and Saints,
and you, my brothers and sisters,
to pray for me to the Lord our God.

Journal thoughts . . .

Peace

When do you feel most at peace? Write about what peace feels like… It can be a poem, list, prayer or, your rambling ideas.

Collection of Grace

Canticle of Simeon

Also called Nunc Dimittis, this portion of "Night Prayer" is from Luke 2:29-32

Lord, now you let your servant go in peace;
your word has been fulfilled.

My own eyes have seen the salvation
which you have prepared in the sight of every people:

A light to reveal you to the nations
and the glory of your people Israel.

Restful Night

Night prayer from Liturgy of the Hours holds some of the most beautiful prayers, including this one.

May the all-powerful Lord grant us a restful night
and a peaceful death.

Protect us, Lord, as we stay awake;
watch over us as we sleep,
that awake, we may keep watch with Christ,
and asleep, rest in his peace.

My *Flexible* Plan

Write down the things that will help you at this season of your life to connect with God throughout the day. You can include page numbers or prayer titles. If a category does not seem to apply to you, skip it.

How will I connect with God throughout the day?

❑ Morning:

❑ Continually:

❑ Mealtime:

❑ Specific Activities:

❑ Evening/Bedtime:

❑ Other Ideas:

Dear God, I want to connect with you throughout the day, especially...

In order to help me connect, I will remember the words...

My habits may need to change a little bit by...

This is about a relationship with you. I can see...

Love,

Chapter 3

Meditating

This is the thing I am most likely to let go of when I am stressed. Even right now as I write this book, I am tempted to skip today's time in quiet prayer and meditation. But it is like skipping a friend's party or going to bed without saying good night to a loved one – a good relationship can usually handle it but those are the treasured moments we do not want to miss. Golden moments where memories are made and hearts are warmed.

I began those Golden moments when the dark and starry sky beckoned me as a teen to climb out my bedroom window and linger on the roof of my parents' garage. With wonder and reverence (or sometimes agony and longing), I regularly encountered God on that rooftop.

For years, this image is what I would return to daily (or almost daily) when I would go into prayer. Whether on my bed or at a desk, on a walk or in a church, I would encounter God with heart to heart. I would step into a moment of wonder. But now adays, I often step into an empty silence. My heart is less tumultuous and God's presence is less surprising. Now, it is a moment of domestic love. A simple faithfulness. My humble acknowledgment of God and his humble acknowledgment of me. Perhaps next season it will take a different tone. Your prayer times too will wax and wane in their felt experience. God never wastes a moment. All of it matters. All of it means something. He brings us on a journey and the scenery changes. We too change, from one glory to another.

You are made for heaven. A taste of it comes through meditation. When you deeply reflect on who God is and spend time letting God love you, an enduring peace begins. It comes through both the work of God and the active surrender of the person. Meditation is like sunshine for a garden.

The first section of this chapter will give you frameworks for how to meditate/ reflect. The rest of the sections offer things to use during your time of meditation.

When you hear the word "meditation" you may have in mind some variation of what a Buddhist, Hindu, therapist or yoga instructor means. These beautiful practices are not the same as Christian meditation – although they have similarities.

The goal of Christian meditation is love.

In this book, I use the words prayer, meditation, reflection, prayer-time, and devotion interchangeably.

Given what you found in the reading on this page,

What is prayer?

Explain (more than just a list) at least three aspects of it.

Formats for Meditations

Every day we can turn to God to guide, comfort and sustain us. Ten to sixty minutes of dedicated reflection/meditation each day will certainly bear fruit! In order to get a basis for our times of prayer, meditation and reflection, let us consider what prayer actually is.

The Catechism of the Catholic Church on Prayer

"For me, prayer is a surge of the heart; it is a simple look turned toward heaven, it is a cry of recognition and of love, embracing both trial and joy."[1]

Prayer as God's gift
2559 "Prayer is the raising of one's mind and heart to God or the requesting of good things from God."[2] ...He who humbles himself will be exalted;[4] *humility* is the foundation of prayer. Only when we humbly acknowledge that "we do not know how to pray as we ought,"[5] are we ready to receive freely the gift of prayer. "Man is a beggar before God."[6]

2560 "If you knew the gift of God!"[7] The wonder of prayer is revealed beside the well where we come seeking water: there, Christ comes to meet every human being. It is he who first seeks us and asks us for a drink. Jesus thirsts; his asking arises from the depths of God's desire for us. Whether we realize it or not, prayer is the encounter of God's thirst with ours. God thirsts that we may thirst for him.[8]

Prayer as covenant
2562 ... According to Scripture, it is the *heart* that prays...

2563 The heart is the dwelling-place where I am, where I live; according to the Semitic or Biblical expression, the heart is the place "to which I withdraw." The heart is our hidden center, beyond the grasp of our reason and of others; only the Spirit of God can fathom the human heart and know it fully.

Prayer as communion
2565 ... the life of prayer is the habit of being in the presence of the thrice-holy God and in communion with him.

Lectio Divina

Lectio divina is a slow, contemplative praying of the Scriptures that Christians have practiced for many centuries. Sometimes in lectio divina, you may return several times to the printed text; at other times, only a single word or phrase will fill the whole time. Lectio divina has no goal other than that of being in the presence of God by praying the Scriptures. Here is a guide using the words of Pope Benedict XVI in his Apostolic Exhortation, <u>Verbum Domini</u>.

Lectio- "It opens with the reading (Lectio) of a text, which leads to a desire to understand its true content: what does the biblical text say in itself? Without this, there is always a risk that the text will become a pretext for never moving beyond our own ideas"(VD 87)

Meditatio- Next comes meditation (Meditatio), which asks: what does the biblical text say to us? Here, each person, individually but also as a member of the community, must let himself or herself be moved and challenged (VD 87).

Oratio- Following this, comes prayer (Oratio), which asks the question: what do we say to the Lord in response to his word? Prayer, as petition, intercession, thanksgiving and praise, is the primary way by which the word transforms us (VD 87).

Contemplatio- Next comes contemplation (Contemplatio), during which we take up, as a gift from God, his own way of seeing and judging reality, and ask ourselves what conversion of mind, heart and life is the Lord asking of us? […] Contemplation aims at creating within us a truly wise and discerning vision of reality, as God sees it, and at forming within us "the mind of Christ" (1Cor 2:16)" (VD 87).

Actio- The process of Lectio Divina is not concluded until it arrives at action (Actio), which moves the believer to make his or her life a gift for others in charity. We find the supreme synthesis and fulfillment of this process in the Mother of God. For every member of the faithful Mary is the model of docile acceptance of God's word, for she "kept all these things, pondering them in her heart" (Lk 2:19; cf. 2:51)" (VD 87).

Lectio Divina can seem confusing at first. Putting it in your own words can make a simpler "go-to" for your own prayer. Describe each step in a way that make sense to you.

Words that Make Sense

Lectio-

Meditatio-

Oratio-

Contemplatio-

Actio-

Visio Divina

You can take this same technique (page 46) and think about a scene from the bible using an image.

Find a picture that helps you to think about a scene from the life of Jesus. If you are using a digital version of this book, paste the image below:

Ignatian Scripture Reading

Saint Ignatius of Loyola was a master of imagination. He taught people to interact with the Lord (called colloquy) while reading Scripture and using the imagination. The words below are my own summary of the Ignatian style of Scripture reading that I learned at Loyola University.

1. Get in a comfortable position and relax. Try to let go of anxieties and random thoughts.

2. The idea is to really place yourself within the Scripture story- to place yourself in the scene. With the first read, set the scene in your mind. Then, just begin to notice things. Observe what is happening in the scene. Just notice what you see, hear, smell and feel. If something in your imagination or a word hits you, don't ignore it- stay with that.

   Consider: What is the scene like? Where are you? Are you an active or passive participant? Did you communicate with others? Is there anything that surprised you that you thought of, heard or saw?

3. Read the passage again. Become a part of the story. As you experience the story again, imagine yourself there and notice how you interact with Jesus and how Jesus interacts with you. The only "rule" for your imagination/prayer is that you cannot be Jesus. The reason for this is that the goal of this type of Scripture listening or reading is to interact with Christ and see how he wants to encourage you, challenge you or teach you. Listen to his words of encouragement to you or see him face to face.

   Consider: Did you feel resistance toward anything? What is God saying to you? If something stands out to you, what is it that draws you to that word, image or phrase?

4. Give thanks for the graces your received in prayer. Pray for the help to act upon them.

Observation/ Interpretation/ Application

This type of reading Scripture is common among both Catholics and Protestants. After a few times of looking at a passage this way, the three-fold approach becomes fairly natural. In order to be more engaged, sometimes it is helpful to write down your answers to each stage.

Observe - What does the text say?
What is this passage about?
What is the main theme?
What words or phrases or concepts are repeated?
What are the cause and effect relationships? Contrasts? Commands?
What type of literature are you reading (Gospel, letter, history, wisdom?)
Who is the author? The audience? What was the situation?

Interpret - What does it mean?
What does this passage mean?
Ask, what does this say about God's character (who God is)?
What does this say about the human condition (who we are)?
How does this passage fit in with the heartbeat of the Christian message?
Because of the observations, what can I infer?

Apply - How does this passage apply to me?
Which part can I relate to?
What am I challenged by?
What is encouraging?
What stands out?
What can I do this week in response?

Try it!

Pick a passage from the bible – perhaps Psalm 1. Use this method from page 47 and write down your observations, interpretations, and applications.

Observe

Interpret

Apply

Our feelings greatly affect our behavior but sometimes we are not aware of what those feelings are unless we consciously evaluate them. This is true about religious and prayer as well. There are no right or wrong answers below – they are just feelings. Feeling any of them are completely fine. Once you realize your feelings, you can choose how you want to respond, continue, think, etc.

How are you feeling about prayer and meditation?

Mark all that apply

- ❑ Intrigued
- ❑ Sleepy
- ❑ Attracted to it
- ❑ Forced into this
- ❑ Overwhelmed
- ❑ Confused
- ❑ I don't have enough time
- ❑ I like the guidance
- ❑ Seems too personal
- ❑ Familiar in a good way
- ❑ I can't concentrate
- ❑ Peaceful
- ❑ I am comforted
- ❑ I want to love God
- ❑ Blank – it's hard to think
- ❑ Restful
- ❑ Glad –it puts life in perspective
- ❑ Normal - it's just being w/ God

St. Josemaria's Prayer Before Personal Meditation

Every time I've heard a priest from Opus Dei give a reflection/talk to a group, he has always begun with this prayer. It is also very helpful before a personal prayer time.

My Lord and my God,
I firmly believe that you are here,
that you see me,
that you hear me.

I adore you with profound reverence;
I ask you for pardon of my sins
and grace to make this time
of prayer fruitful.

My Mother Immaculate,
Saint Joseph, my Father and Lord,
my Guardian Angel, intercede for me.

St. Josemaria's Prayer After Personal Meditation

If you do not have a devotion to St. Joseph, I think that the end of this prayer is a little awkward to pray and could easily be omitted. If you are curious though, you could do a little research about why St. Josemaria was so devoted to St. Joseph.

I give you thanks, my God,
for the good resolutions, affections and inspirations that you have communicated to me in this meditation.
I ask you for help to put them into effect.

My Mother Immaculate,
Saint Joseph, my Father and Lord,
my Guardian Angel, intercede for me.

Reflection Content Ideas

Many of the following prayers or ideas can be used for your time of personal prayer.

Memory Verses

One way to let the Word of God dwell within you is to memorize it. Keeping a paper verse in your pocket, setting a challenge with friends and posting verses around your house can help quite a bit. Amazing things happen when you memorize Scripture. Also, you can use these for your prayer time. .

Romans 8:38-39
For I am convinced that neither death, nor life, nor angels, nor principalities, nor present things, nor future things, nor powers, nor height, nor depth, nor any other creature will be able to separate us from the love of God in Christ Jesus our Lord.

Matthew 11:28-30
Come to me, all you who labor and are burdened, and I will give you rest. Take my yoke upon you and learn from me, for I am meek and humble of heart; and you will find rest for yourselves. For my yoke is easy, and my burden light.

Philippians 4:13
I have the strength for everything through him who empowers me.

Psalm 27:1
The Lord is my light and my salvation; whom should I fear? The Lord is my life's refuge; of whom should I be afraid?

Jeremiah 29:11
For I know well the plans I have in mind for you—oracle of the Lord—plans for your welfare and not for woe, so as to give you a future of hope.

Lamentations 3:22-23
The Lord's acts of mercy are not exhausted,
his compassion is not spent;
They are renewed each morning.

2 Corinthians 4:18
We look not to what is seen but to what is unseen; for what is seen is transitory, but what is unseen is eternal.

Reminds me...

What memory do these verses remind you of? Pick a bible verse from page 49-52 and associate it with some experience that you have gone through in the past. Write your story of that memory:

Tough Situation

The word of God can speak into our own lives. What situation do you have that is difficult right now? Summarize it here:

Collection of Grace

Proverbs 3:5-7
Trust in the Lord with all your heart, on your own intelligence do not rely; In all your ways be mindful of him, and he will make straight your paths.

Galatians 2:20
Yet I live, no longer I, but Christ lives in me; insofar as I now live in the flesh, I live by faith in the Son of God who has loved me and given himself up for me.

James 1:22
Be doers of the word and not hearers only, deluding yourselves.

Colossians 3:23
Whatever you do, do from the heart, as for the Lord and not for others.

1 Corinthians 15:58
Therefore, my beloved brothers, be firm, steadfast, always fully devoted to the work of the Lord, knowing that in the Lord your labor is not in vain.

James 4:7
Submit yourselves to God. Resist the devil, and he will flee from you.

Luke 16:13
No servant can serve two masters. He will either hate one and love the other, or be devoted to one and despise the other. You cannot serve God and mammon.

1 John 4:7-8
Beloved, let us love one another, because love is of God; everyone who loves is begotten by God and knows God. Whoever is without love does not know God, for God is love.

Hebrews 12:1-2
Therefore, since we are surrounded by so great a cloud of witnesses, let us rid ourselves of every burden and sin that clings to us and persevere in running the race that lies before us while keeping our eyes fixed on Jesus, the leader and perfecter of faith. For the sake of the joy that lay before him he endured the cross, despising its shame, and has taken his seat at the right of the throne of God.

Acts 1:8
You will receive power when the holy Spirit comes upon you, and you will be my witnesses in Jerusalem, throughout Judea and Samaria, and to the ends of the earth.

Romans 12:1-2
I urge you therefore, brothers, by the mercies of God, to offer your bodies as a living sacrifice, holy and pleasing to God, your spiritual worship. Do not conform yourselves to this age but be transformed by the renewal of your mind, that you may discern what is the will of God, what is good and pleasing and perfect.

1 Thessalonians 5:18
In all circumstances give thanks, for this is the will of God for you in Christ Jesus.

Philippians 4:6-7
Have no anxiety at all, but in everything, by prayer and petition, with thanksgiving, make your requests known to God. Then the peace of God that surpasses all understanding will guard your hearts and minds in Christ Jesus.

Psalm 119:105
Your word is a lamp for my feet, a light for my path.

Hebrews 4:16
Let us confidently approach the throne of grace to receive mercy and to find grace for timely help.

1 John 1:9
If we acknowledge our sins, he is faithful and just and will forgive our sins and cleanse us from every wrongdoing.

James 5:16
Therefore, confess your sins to one another and pray for one another, that you may be healed. The fervent prayer of a righteous person is very powerful.

Micah 6:8
You have been told, O mortal, what is good, and what the Lord requires of you: Only to do justice and to love goodness, and to walk humbly with your God.

Perhaps there is a bible verse that can bring you some comfort, wisdom, strength, or courage as you go through this situation. Look through pages 49-52 and determine which verse will help you the most. Rewrite it in your own words:

a verse to help

A Gift

A bible verse is a good way to encourage people. List some people you know (young or old) who would be encouraged by some of these verses. Write the verse citation (ex: Isaiah 55:2) next to the person's name.

Name   **Verse**

_____

_____

_____

_____

_____

Collection of Grace

Matthew 25:40
Amen, I say to you, whatever you did for one of these least brothers of mine, you did for me.

Matthew 28:19-20
Go, therefore, and make disciples of all nations, baptizing them in the name of the Father, and of the Son, and of the Holy Spirit, teaching them to observe all that I have commanded you. And behold, I am with you always, until the end of the age.

Isaiah 55:2
Why spend your money for what is not bread; your wages for what does not satisfy? Only listen to me, and you shall eat well, you shall delight in rich fare.

Ephesians 6:12
For our struggle is not with flesh and blood but with the principalities, with the powers, with the world rulers of this present darkness, with the evil spirits in the heavens.

Isaiah 54:13
All your children shall be taught by the Lord; great shall be the peace of your children.

1 Samuel 16:7
The Lord sees not as man sees; man looks on the outward appearance, but the Lord looks on the heart.

Joshua 1:9
Do not fear nor be dismayed, for the Lord, your God, is with you wherever you go.

Isaiah 54:10
Though the mountains fall away and the hills be shaken, my love shall never fall away from you nor my covenant of peace be shaken, says the Lord, who has mercy on you.

Isaiah 55:6
Seek the Lord while he may be found, call upon him while he is near.

2 Corinthians 12:9
He said to me, "My grace is sufficient for you, for power is made perfect in weakness." I will rather boast most gladly of my weaknesses, in order that the power of Christ may dwell with me.

Matthew 5:16
Just so, your light must shine before others, that they may see your good deeds and glorify your heavenly Father.

Parables

Jesus often spoke in short stories which have a little bit of shock to them. See yourself in them and ask the Lord about their meaning.

The Lamp under a Bushel
- Matthew 5:14–15, Mark 4:21–25, Luke 8:16–18
Parable of the Good Samaritan
- Luke 10:25–37
The Rich Fool
- Luke 12:16–21
The House on the Rock
- Matthew 7:24–27, Luke 6:46–49
New Wine into Old Wineskins
- Matthew 9:16–17, Mark 2:21–22, Luke 5:37–39
Parable of the Sower
- Matthew 13:3–9, Mark 4:3–9, Luke 8:5–8
The Barren Fig Tree
- Luke 13:6–9
Parable of the Mustard Seed
- Matthew 13:31–32, Mark 4:30–32, Luke 13:18–19
The Leaven
- Matthew 13:33–33, Luke 13:20–21
Parable of the Pearl
- Matthew 13:45–46
The Lost Sheep
- Matthew 18:10–14, Luke 15:4–6
The Lost Coin
- Luke 15:8–9
Parable of the Prodigal Son
- Luke 15:11–32
Rich Man and Lazarus
- Luke 16:19–31
The Workers in the Vineyard
- Matthew 20:1–16
The Great Banquet
- Matthew 22:1–14, Luke 14:15–24
The Ten Virgins
- Matthew 25:1–13
The Sheep and the Goats
- Matthew 25:31–46

Reminds me...

Any of these parables would be good passages to read with the bible study techniques listed on page 45, 46 or 47. Try one and jot some notes about it:

Favorite spot

If you have 15 minutes free time to pray, think and read, where do you go? Draw or describe your zone.

Carrie's Ideas of Things to Do During a Prayer Time

The most important thing to do during prayer is to <u>love.</u> The feelings or insights you have are much less important that your act of love to God. With that in mind, the sky is the limit. Here are some ideas in case you ever get stuck or need a change.

- With Jesus, read, think and talk about part of the Gospel, New Testament, or any part of the Bible. Go slowly.

- Find a Psalm or part of a Psalm that hits home and read it to God.

- Get a bible study book and fill out the answers.

- Make a resolution. Think through your motivations for this and your aids in following through. Follow the Holy Spirit.

- Reflectively read a spiritual book and converse with Jesus about it.

- Read through the prayers of some saints – its what other people have whispered in their personal prayer times.

- Lift up your family to God. Imagine that you are standing next to them and you are all right before the throne of God. Smile at the Lord and show him your people.

- List on paper, or mentally, people in your life. Let your list be your prayer for them.

- Think deeply with God about the people in your life. Pray for their needs and hopes. Ask God how you can help. What do you need to know about them which will help you to love and serve like Christ?

- With God, list your responsibilities. Tell Him what you are having the most trouble with. Note the ideas that come to mind as solutions.

- Sit with Jesus and discuss life.

- Go for a walk with Jesus.

- Just be quiet.

- Lie down and hide yourself in God's arms. Let go of your troubles. Trust in the Lord. Let your breath speak His name.

- Write down what you think God is asking of you at this point of life. Ask Him.

- Cast all your cares on him because he cares for you. Start a temper tantrum and listen to God as he loves you through it. Respond to him.

- Dedicate your body in service to the Lord as you stretch.

- Find an emotional wound and show it to God. Sit with it for a while.

- Let go of something.

- If you are struggling to find a place alone or undistracted to pray and let your thoughts roll on to God, try the shower, the car or even your bed when others give you the peace and privacy to sleep.

- Thumb through a spiritual book you've read already and think in God's presence about what you learned.

- Write down a few quotes from a spiritual book you've read. Ask God what it means for your life.

- Is your mind swimming with things you need to do? Write them down. What are your feelings about these tasks? Speak with God about it. Ask God what you need to do. Envision yourself accomplishing these tasks with Jesus by your side. As you look over your list, what does it reveal about your own deeper desires? Journal or speak with God about these things.

- What is the Father's will for you this week? Ask the Holy Spirit to accomplish it in you.

You are in charge

Imagine that you are volunteering at church to help lead a week of camp for 5th graders. They already had games, skits and a few talks. You are in charge of the 10-minute prayer time in the chapel, just before a break for snacks. The kids are really loving the camp and feel open, happy and eager about this day which is bringing them so much love. How would you direct the 10 minutes of prayer for them? Write it down.

Is this something you would like to do on your own prayer time?

 Yes   No   ☐ Maybe

What toy, place, person, event, or food do you like so much that you could go on and on, talking about it's good features?

List some of those good things.

This is a bit similar to praise. In praise, you enter into contemplation of how good God is

and **you express it.**

What is one thing that needs to change for you to more freely express your praise to God?

Praise

When I learned to praise God, I learned to be joyful. To praise and worship is to outwardly admit that God is God. It is usually done with gladness because the people offering praise realize that this beautiful, powerful, infinite God is with them, on their side and comes in love. Praise is a lively way to meditate.

Psalm 95

This is the psalm most people in religious orders pray first thing in the morning.

Come, let us sing to the Lord
and shout with joy to the Rock who saves us.
Let us approach him with praise and thanksgiving
and sing joyful songs to the Lord.

The Lord is God, the mighty God,
the great king over all the gods.
He holds in his hands the depths of the earth
and the highest mountains as well.
He made the sea; it belongs to him,
the dry land, too, for it was formed by his hands.

Come, then, let us bow down and worship,
bending the knee before the Lord, our maker.
For he is our God and we are his people,
the flock he shepherds.

Today, listen to the voice of the Lord:
Do not grow stubborn, as your fathers did
in the wilderness,
when at Meriba and Massah
they challenged me and provoked me,
Although they had seen all of my works.

Psalm 67

O God, be gracious and bless us
and let your face shed its light upon us.
So will your ways be known upon earth
and all nations learn your saving help.

Let the peoples praise you, O God;
let all the peoples praise you.

Let the nations be glad and exult
for you rule the world with justice.
With fairness you rule the peoples,
you guide the nations on earth.

Let the peoples praise you, O God;
let all the peoples praise you.

The earth has yielded its fruit
for God, our God, has blessed us.
May God still give us his blessing
till the ends of the earth revere him. s

Psalm 100

Here is a happy psalm of praise from the Divine Office.

Cry out with joy to the Lord, all the earth.
Serve the Lord with gladness.
Come before him, singing for joy.

Know that he, the Lord, is God.
He made us, we belong to him,
we are his people, the sheep of his flock.

Go within his gates, giving thanks.
Enter his courts with songs of praise.
Give thanks to him and bless his name.

Indeed, how good is the Lord,
eternal his merciful love.
He is faithful from age to age.

Analogy of Imagery

The psalmists used imagery from what they saw around them in order to express their gratitude and understanding of God. Identify three images from the psalms on page 56 or 57.

1.

2.

3.

What images would you use from your environment to do the same? Write about or draw three images.

Can you handle silence?

Silence is a powerful place to meet God but it can be hard to ease out of the noise of our lives. Do you ever intentionally avoid it? Check the box next to the things you do to distract you from silence.

- ❑ Social media
- ❑ Eat
- ❑ Be busy
- ❑ Find someone to be near
- ❑ Watch t.v.
- ❑ Listen to music
- ❑ Pick a fight with someone
- ❑ Play video games
- ❑ Message a friend

Why do you think silence is hard?

What good might come on the other side of pushing through the difficulty?

Te Deum

We celebrate with this prayer on Sundays and holy seasons like Easter and Christmas.

You are God: we praise you;
You are the Lord: we acclaim you;
You are the eternal Father:
All creation worships you.

To you all angels, all the powers of heaven,
Cherubim and Seraphim, sing in endless praise:
Holy, holy, holy Lord, God of power and might,
heaven and earth are full of your glory.

The glorious company of apostles praise you.
The noble fellowship of prophets praise you.
The white-robed army of martyrs praise you.

Throughout the world the holy Church acclaims you;
Father, of majesty unbounded,
your true and only Son, worthy of all worship,
and the Holy Spirit, advocate and guide.

You, Christ, are the king of glory,
the eternal Son of the Father.
When you became man to set us free
you did not shun the Virgin's womb.

You overcame the sting of death
and opened the kingdom of heaven to all believers.
You are seated at God's right hand in glory.
We believe that you will come and be our judge.

Come then, Lord, and help your people,
bought with the price of your own blood,
and bring us with your saints
to glory everlasting.

From the Heart – Praising with Abandonment
Praising God with your whole heart is like living in heaven for a moment. Here is a way you can praise God on your own.

I love you, God, you are…
God, you have given me…
Praise you, Jesus!
You are worthy of praise because…
You are my…

Praise Ideas

Try other prayers for praise throughout this book.

Tell God about your love for him.
Repeat a line from a psalm over and over.
Tell God the attributes you notice about him.
Sing praise songs to him.
Make up a song spontaneously.
Play an instrument to him.
Listen to music about God.
Lift up your hands in love and awe.
Lie down and physically open your arms to God.
Ask God to fill you with his Holy Spirit so you can praise.
Silently "look" at God.
Adore Jesus in the Blessed Sacrament.

Try it!

Try one of the ideas for praise listed on page 59. Draw an arrow to the choice you made.

Write about your praise time.

Read the peace prayer of Saint Francis.

What kind of an instrument are you?

Consider what kind of an effect you have in your family, work, friends, school, etc.

Circle, draw or write the instrument that represents you at your best. Put a square around one that represents you at a low.

Explain.

Devotions of the Saints

(and other holy people)
These prayers reflect a depth of love for God that I wouldn't be able to express on my own. I use them in my own time of reflection or for morning or bedtime prayers.

Peace Prayer of St. Francis

This popular prayer brings a humble perspective to every human encounter and in the midst of it, brings peace.

Lord, make me an instrument of your peace:
where there is hatred, let me sow love;
where there is injury, pardon;
where there is doubt, faith;
where there is despair, hope;
where there is darkness, light;
where there is sadness, joy.

O divine Master, grant that I may not so much seek
to be consoled as to console,
to be understood as to understand,
to be loved as to love.
For it is in giving that we receive,
it is in pardoning that we are pardoned,
and it is in dying that we are born to eternal life.

Nada te Turbe by St. Teresa of Avila

This is actually a poem, not a prayer but it still is wonderful to internalize through meditation. I imagine she encouraged herself with these words since it was found handwritten in her hymnal.

Let nothing disturb you ,
Let nothing frighten you,
All things are passing away.
God never changes.
Patience obtains all things.
Whoever has God lacks nothing;
God alone suffices.

The Holy Face

Devotion to the Holy Face of Jesus has brought many miracles. This particular prayer was composed by Blessed Maria Pierina De Micheli.

O Blessed Face of my kind Savior,
by the tender love
and piercing sorrow
of Our Lady as she beheld You
In Your cruel Passion,
grant us to share
in this intense sorrow and love
so as to fulfill the holy will of God
to the utmost of our ability.

The Anima Christi

Saint Ignatius used this prayer in the beginning of the Spiritual Exercises.

Soul of Christ, sanctify me;
Body of Christ, save me;
Blood of Christ, inebriate me;
Water from Christ's side, wash me.
Passion of Christ, strengthen me;
O good Jesus, hear me;
Within Thy wounds hide me;
Suffer me not to be separated from Thee.
From the malicious enemy defend me;
In the hour of my death call me,
And bid me come unto Thee,
That I may praise Thee with Thy saints
and with Thy angels
Forever and ever.

Blood of Christ, inebriate me

inebriate

transitive verb

1: to make drunk : INTOXICATE
2: to exhilarate or stupefy as if by liquor

Keywords

Complete the crossword puzzle and let the key words echo in your mind.

1. To get up in the morning
2. Something attached to your arm
3. Giving a lot
4. The second person of the Trinity
5. God in three persons
6. Someone who stands to protect
7. Forces away arrows
8. To keep safe from attack

Saint Patrick's Prayer

The entire prayer attributed to St. Patrick is much longer. This portion of it is great for a morning offering.

I arise today, through
God's strength to pilot me,
God's might to uphold me,
God's wisdom to guide me,
God's eye to look before me,
God's ear to hear me,
God's word to speak for me,
God's hand to guard me,
God's shield to protect me,
God's host to save me.

Christ with me, Christ before me, Christ behind me,
Christ in me, Christ beneath me, Christ above me,
Christ on my right, Christ on my left,
Christ when I lie down, Christ when I sit down,
Christ in the heart of every man who thinks of me,
Christ in the mouth of every man who speaks of me,
Christ in the eye that sees me,
Christ in the ear that hears me.

I arise today through a mighty strength,
the invocation of the Trinity,
Through belief in the Threeness,
Through confession of the Oneness
of the Creator of creation.

Prayer for Generosity

This is attributed to St. Ignatius of Loyola. A football team at a nearby Jesuit high school used to pray this before every practice.

Lord, teach me to be generous.
Teach me to serve you as you deserve;
to give and not to count the cost,
to fight and not to heed the wounds,
to toil and not to seek for rest,
to labor and not to ask for reward,
save that of knowing that I do your will.

Suscipe

I prayed this wonderful act of surrender, attributed to St. Ignatius of Loyola, over and over when I was discerning what to do with my life. I still need to pray it!

Take, Lord, and receive all my liberty,
my memory, my understanding,
and my entire will,
all I have and call my own.
You have given all to me.
To you, Lord, I return it.
Everything is yours; do with it what you will.
Give me only your love and your grace,
that is enough for me.

Prayer of St. Charles de Foucauld

This prayer was composed shortly before St. Charles de Foucauld was martyred!

Father, I abandon myself into your hands;
do with me what you will.
Whatever you may do, I thank you:
I am ready for all, I accept all.

Let only your will be done in me,
and in all your creatures.
I wish no more than this, O Lord.

Into your hands I commend my soul:
I offer it to you with all the love of my heart,
for I love you, Lord,
and so need to give myself,
to surrender myself into your hands
without reserve,
and with boundless confidence,
for you are my Father.

Abandonment/ Surrender

These words can sometimes have a negative feeling – like someone was uncared for or lost. In the instance of these prayers, however, it is almost the opposite.

It takes **trust** – confidence in the good intention and ability of the one you are handing things over to.

What are some things that you can surrender to God? List them in the gift boxes.

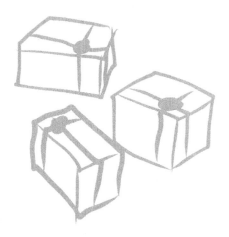

My Lord
God, I have
no idea
where I am
going.

- Thomas Merton

Collection of Grace

Prayer of St. Thomas More

Certainly, there are a lot of good personal qualities to pray for here.

O Lord, give us a mind that is humble,
quiet, peaceable, patient and charitable,
and a taste of your Holy Spirit
in all our thoughts, words and deeds.

O Lord, give us a lively faith,
a firm hope, a fervent charity, a love of you.
Take from us all lukewarmness in meditation,
and all dullness in prayer.

Give us fervour and delight in thinking of you,
your grace, and your tender compassion toward us.
Give us, good Lord, the grace to work for
the things we pray for.

Thomas Merton Prayer

Lots of people turn to this prayer when they are in the midst of life changes - especially young adults, so, I was surprised when my husband's grandmother asked for a copy of it. I suppose you are never too old to put all your trust in God and ask him to lead you.

My Lord God, I have no idea where I am going.
I do not see the road ahead of me.
I cannot know for certain where it will end.
Nor do I really know myself,
and the fact that I think that I am following your will
does not mean that I am actually doing so.
But I believe that the desire to please you does in fact please you.
And I hope I have that desire in all that I am doing.
I hope that I will never do anything apart from that desire.
And I know that if I do this you will lead me by the right road
though I may know nothing about it.
Therefore, will I trust you always
though I may seem to be lost and in the shadow of death.
I will not fear, for you are ever with me,
and you will never leave me to face my perils alone.

St. John Vianney

Obviously, this saint was full of love. I imagine that this prayer was not only born out of feeling but also out of faith.

I love You, O my God,
and my only desire is to love You
until the last breath of my life.
I love You, O my infinitely lovable God,
and I would rather die loving You,
than live without loving You.
I love You, Lord, and the only grace I ask
is to love You eternally.
My God, if my tongue cannot say in every moment
that I love You,
I want my heart to repeat it to You
as often as I draw breath.

Serenity Prayer

When I was growing up, my mom had this prayer by Reinhold Niebuhr posted right by the kitchen sink. I suppose we drove her to reach for serenity!

God, grant me the serenity
to accept the things I cannot change,
the courage to change the things I can,
and the wisdom to know the difference.

Living one day at a time,
enjoying one moment at a time;
accepting hardship as a pathway to peace;
taking, as Jesus did,
this sinful world as it is,
not as I would have it;
trusting that You will make all things right
if I surrender to Your will;
so that I may be reasonably happy in this life
and supremely happy with You forever in the next.

Serenity and Courage

There are some difficult things in life that you cannot change (although they may change without you). We need peace and serenity in the midst of them.

What are these difficult things in your life? Write four in the peace sign.

There are other difficult things that can be changed but, courage is needed. Write one of these things in the burst below.

Let your pure love imprint Your image so **deeply** upon my heart that I shall never be able to forget You.

The prayers of the saints often have a theme of trusting God so much that they entirely give themselves to him. Part of this is because they experienced Jesus in their lives at some point. Some of them continued to feel God and some did not. All of them could look with faith and see his presence and then trust.

Would you like this kind of trust? Pray about it now.

❑ Yes   ❑ No   ❑ Maybe

An Act of Consecration to The Sacred Heart of Jesus

At a time when the culture was very harsh, the Holy Spirit inspired St. Margarete Mary Alacoque to foster a devotion to the Sacred Heart of Jesus so that we can more intimately understand love.

I give myself and consecrate
to the Sacred Heart of our Lord Jesus Christ,
my person and my life, my actions, pains and sufferings,
so that I may be unwilling to make use of any part of my being
other than to honor, love and glorify the Sacred Heart.
This is my unchanging purpose, namely, to be all His,
and to do all things for the love of Him,
at the same time renouncing with all my heart
whatever is displeasing to Him.
I therefore take You, O Sacred Heart,
to be the only object of my love,
the guardian of my life,
my assurance of salvation,
the remedy of my weakness and inconstancy,
the atonement for all the faults of my life
and my sure refuge at the hour of death.

Be then, O Heart of goodness,
my justification before God the Father,
and turn away from me the strokes of his righteous anger.
O Heart of love, I put all my confidence in You,
for I fear everything from my own wickedness and frailty,
but I hope for all things from Your goodness and bounty.

or resist Your holy will;
let Your pure love imprint Your image so deeply upon my heart,
that I shall never be able to forget You
or to be separated from You.
May I obtain from all Your loving kindness
the grace of having my name written in Your Heart,
for in You I desire to place all my happiness and glory,
living and dying in bondage to You.

Patient Trust

This encouragement from Teilhard de Chardin can help us be patient as we grow into the people God is forming us to be.

Above all, trust in the slow work of God.
We are quite naturally impatient in everything
to reach the end without delay.
We should like to skip the intermediate stages.
We are impatient of being on the way to something
unknown, something new.
And yet it is the law of all progress
that it is made by passing through
some stages of instability—
and that it may take a very long time.

And so I think it is with you;
your ideas mature gradually—let them grow,
let them shape themselves, without undue haste.
Don't try to force them on,
as though you could be today what time
(that is to say, grace and circumstances
acting on your own good will)
will make of you tomorrow.

Only God could say what this new spirit
gradually forming within you will be.
Give Our Lord the benefit of believing
that his hand is leading you,
and accept the anxiety of feeling yourself
in suspense and incomplete.

 ### From the Heart – Expressing your Love
It is good and healthy for our relationship to frequently express our devotion to God.

You can express your love to God similar to the way that you love people. It takes time together, acts of service, words of affirmation, physical touch and gifts. God loves to receive your love. Go ahead, tell him that you love him!

Read the advice from Teilhard de Chardin.
What mental or emotion actions does it lead you to take? In other words, what good things do you want to keep in mind from this poem?

If a friend were to give you a framed picture with one of these quotes about **contemplation** to go on your wall, which one would you want?

Draw an arrow.

St. Teresa of Avila on Contemplation

I have found quite a bit of freedom by reading St. Teresa's experiences of prayer. She has an interesting mix of intimacy, faithful duty and passivity. Maybe you will be inspired by her to open your prayer into new realms. To know how a person should pray, she pays quite a bit of attention to what stage a person is in and what Jesus is doing in the person's inner life.

All one need do is go into solitude and look at Him within oneself, and not turn away from so good a Guest but with great humility speak to Him as a father. Beseech Him as you would a father; tell him all about your trials; ask Him for a remedy against them, realizing that you are not worthy to be His daughter.

Contemplative prayer [oracion mental] in my opinion is nothing else than a close sharing between friends; it means taking time frequently to be alone with him who we know loves us.

Contemplative prayer seeks him "whom my soul loves."

It is Jesus, and in him, the Father. We seek him, because to desire him is always the beginning of love, and we seek him in that pure faith which causes us to be born of him and to live in him. In this inner prayer we can still meditate, but our attention is fixed on the Lord himself.

The important thing is not to think much but to love much; and so do that which best stirs you to love.

This Beloved of ours is merciful and good. Besides, he so deeply longs for our love that he keeps calling us to come closer. This voice of his is so sweet that the poor soul falls apart in the face of her own inability to instantly do whatever he asks of her. And so you can see, hearing him hurts much more than not being able to hear him…

It is of great importance, when we begin to practice prayer, not to let ourselves be frightened by our own thoughts.

My *Flexible* Plan

What kind of prayer times is God leading you to experience? Are there prayers in this section which can help you? Leave aside guilt or anxiety and just follow God leading your life.

How is God leading me to reflect?

❑ My God-given desire for silent time with God:

❑ Times of day quiet prayer is possible:

❑ Types of things to read, pray or write about:

❑ Resources I'll consider using:

❑ Prayers to incorporate:

❑ Help I will need from God:

Dear God, I am the kind of person who finds quiet...

I want to spend time with you by...

When it comes to longer periods of time, I ...

When you think of me, what do you...

Chapter 4

Acting Well

He was drunk. How could he do this? After all his words, witness and prayer. He had been the "star" of our retreat! I was devastated to see the leader of our high school retreat acting like a fool at the winter dance. He had created such warmth and fellowship for us underclassmen. He had seemed to be such a good example of brotherly love and love of God. My classmates and I could not grasp the disparity between professing love, faith and prayer but then acting against it.

But God does. In fact, God's love is not shaken by even our worst moments. His love for my hypocritical classmate did not change. Nor does it change for me when 50x's a day, I am off base. God is not surprised or despondent by our wayward behavior. He loves. He waits. He acts on our behalf. God does not love us because we have certain behavior. God loves us. Period. Never changes, never stops. No matter what.

It is this rock-solid love of God which is our foundation for doing well. It is a way of saying back to our creator, "I love you too." Acting well is a way for us to draw close to the God who already lives within us. God's solid love gives us freedom – not fear. We are free to learn, grow and become through out actions. It is unconditional love which compels us to love unconditionally too. And yet we experience in ourselves and in others that we are broken. Even our own actions need God's animation in order to fulfill the purpose for which we were created. This is where prayer come in! You were made to be a light for the world. When you spend time in prayer letting God love you, a good transformation begins. As the Lord of your life, you can ask him how he wants you to live and what areas of your life need to grow and change. This transformation comes through both the work of God and the action of the person. The fire you experience in prayer will give you the power to live the gospel generously and conversely, as you live heroically, you may experience communion with God in prayer.

This chapter has many parts which can help you to flourish in your actions to others, your behavior and thinking. However, you need to start with this idea, otherwise all teaching and attempts to act well will be agonizing. So, first you need to really, really internalize that:

God loves you no matter what.

Got it?

☐ Yes ☐ No ☐ Sort of

Your positive attitudes make a difference

"Scientists from Stanford University have discovered the brain pathway that directly links a positive attitude with achievement."
https://neuroscience.stanford.edu/

Always Attitudes

All of these attitudes drive towards one thing- to love God. Forming your intention on these attitudes can itself be a prayer. There is nothing official about this list in particular, but it is similar to the ways of St. Josemaria Escriva and other saints.

Childlike Identity

You are a child of God. Your identity shapes everything you do and every way you feel about yourself.

Father, you are always with me and I am loved. I can stay mentally, emotionally, physically and spiritually secure in you. Let me represent you well.

Unity of Life

This is a mindset which simplifies life. Everything, ultimately, is for God. No matter how many varied tasks and roles you have in life – all of them can drive toward one purpose: love God.

Jesus, you said that there is only one thing necessary. Please help all the pieces of my life to be directed to that one truth in you. Let me do what you will, when you will it, in the way that you will, and for the reason that you will.

Alacrity

We respond to God's promptings – whether by commandments and teachings, the sufferings of others or inclinations in prayer. We quickly do the will of God like a little kid eager to please his mom.

Speak, Lord. Your servant is listening. The moment it becomes clear what I should do, help me to do it with love. Let me have joy in all that I do, even in suffering, especially for the sake of those around me. I am confident in your love.

Gratitude

Some say that gratitude is the key to happiness. With it, you can cut through depression, find the path to peace and always have a reason to rejoice.

God, thank you for everything you have given me.

Friendship

We are fellow sojourners with the lovable people around us (even when they do not seem so lovable.) Because of this, our servant hearts are full of genuine love, with eyes for those in need.

Jesus, you served the Father through your love to us. I will to serve. I give you my hands, my mind, my actions and my thoughts for the sake of others.

Vocational Excellence

Being excellent in your work, especially your vocation, is an imitation of God your father. Likewise, you show others a witness of the goodness of God.

I embrace this current state of life as your calling. You have chosen me for this work, at this time and made it holy, powerful and lifegiving. Whether, standing up to injustices, serving quietly or enjoying plenty, let me say "yes" like Mary. Please convert my small, broken attempts into something truly pleasing to you. I hope to give you glory and develop good things for your people.

Freedom

Freedom is the capability to do what is good. We aim to remain (or become) free by being detached from all that would drag us into sin. Through this self-control (or self-gift) we can express our love of God according to our unique characteristics and extend this freedom to others.

Lord, you have given everything for me. Let me remain free and totally yours so that I may give everything to you. I want to make a gift of myself. Thank you for enjoying my expression of self to you.

Evangelism

The love of God burns in our hearts. We overflow with grace and bring others the gifts of God.

God, I desire to spread your good news to everyone and every place I go. Help me to be a beacon of your light in action and word.

Read through pages 72 and 73. Highlight the attitude you would like to work on this week. Pray the prayer listed with it.

When do you need this attitude? List 3 moments during the day when it will be crucial.

1.

2.

3.

Jesus, please form my mindsets.

Listed to the right are the precepts for a full adult in the church. Kids' abilities to follow these lies in the hands of their parents. As people get older, they are more capable of living it out themselves.

Do somethings (or all) on this list seem impossible?
Even rules or precepts are meant to

lead us into a relationship.

So... talk about it. Express your feelings and listen to God, now.

- - - - - - - -

This relationship is more than just two way. It includes other people- the church too.

List 3 other people your relationship with God includes.

1.

2.

3.

Growth in Virtue

In order to be close to God, we need to live the Gospel with heroic generosity (virtue) and have the fire of God within us (prayer). Below are lists of obligations, virtues, prayers and quotes that help to paint a picture of what we are trying to embody.

The Precepts of the Church
For centuries, the church has promulgated a few minimum requirements of activities which help maintain order and culture.

1. Attendance at Mass on Sundays and Holy Days of Obligation
2. Confession of serious sin at least once a year
3. Reception of Holy Communion at least once a year during the Easter season
4. Observance of the days of fast and abstinence
5. Provision for the needs of the Church

Holy Days of Obligation
In addition to every Sunday, these are the special days that all Catholics are obliged to gather to celebrate Mass. In some dioceses, like Chicago, some of these feasts are moved to the closest Sunday.

Mary, Mother of God -	January 1
Ascension Thursday -	Fortieth day after Easter
Assumption of the Virgin Mary -	August 15
All Saints -	November 1
Immaculate Conception -	December 8
Nativity of Our Lord, Jesus Christ -	December 25

Fasting Regulations from the USCCB
Ash Wednesday and Good Friday are obligatory days of fasting.
Fridays during Lent are obligatory days of abstinence from meat.
The norms on fasting are obligatory from age 18 until age 59 and for abstinence from meat from age 14 onwards.
When fasting, a person is permitted to eat one full meal, as well as two smaller meals that together are not equal to a full meal.

Theological Virtues

All virtues are found in God and from these flow all other virtues.

Faith is the theological virtue by which we believe in God and believe all that he has said and revealed to us, and that Holy Church proposes for our belief, because he is truth itself. By faith "man freely commits his entire self to God." - CCC 1814

Hope is the theological virtue by which we desire the kingdom of heaven and eternal life as our happiness, placing our trust in Christ's promises and relying not on our own strength, but on the help of the grace of the Holy Spirit. - CCC 1817

Charity is the theological virtue by which we love God above all things for his own sake, and our neighbor as ourselves for the love of God. - CCC 1822

The Cardinal Virtues

The moral virtues which help us to live well in the world.

Prudence is the virtue that disposes practical reason to discern our true good in every circumstance and to choose the right means of achieving it. - CCC 1806

Justice is the moral virtue that consists in the constant and firm will to give their due to God and neighbor. - CCC 1807

Fortitude is the moral virtue that ensures firmness in difficulties and constancy in the pursuit of the good. - CCC 1808

Temperance is the moral virtue that moderates the attraction of pleasures in order to keep desires at the service of what is honorable. - CCC 1809 (adapted)

A virtue is an habitual and firm disposition to do the good.

- Catechism of the Catholic Church 1803

How can virtues help you?

- ❑ School
- ❑ Relationship with parents
- ❑ Health
- ❑ Image
- ❑ Inner feelings
- ❑ Meeting people
- ❑ Finances
- ❑ Competition
- ❑ Self-control
- ❑ Relationship turmoil
- ❑ Disappointments
- ❑ Achieving goals
- ❑ Other :

Write one or two simple words to sum up for you the blessed happiness of God which is linked to your disposition.

_____

_____

_____

_____

_____

_____

_____

_____

_____

Happiness

Collection of Grace

The Beatitudes

Jesus spoke the beatitudes to encourage his many disciples. Recorded here from Matthew 5:1-12. They can also be found in Luke 6:20-22. You can substitute the word "happy" for blessed.

Blessed are the poor in spirit,
for theirs is the kingdom of heaven.

Blessed are those who mourn,
for they will be comforted.

Blessed are the meek,
for they will inherit the earth.

Blessed are those who hunger and thirst for righteousness,
for they will be filled.

Blessed are the merciful,
for they will receive mercy.

Blessed are the pure in heart,
for they will see God.

Blessed are the peacemakers,
for they will be called children of God.

Blessed are those who are persecuted for righteousness' sake,
for theirs is the kingdom of heaven.

Blessed are you when people revile you and persecute you and utter all kinds of evil against you falsely on my account.

Rejoice and be glad,
for your reward is great in heaven,
for in the same way they persecuted the prophets who were before you.

The Corporal Works of Mercy

Although these are things Christians should do often, it is helpful for my family to focus on them during Lent. They primarily come from the passage about the sheep and the goats in Matthew 25.

To feed the hungry
To give water to the thirsty
To clothe the naked
To shelter the homeless
To visit the sick
To visit the imprisoned, or ransom the captive
To bury the dead

The Spiritual Works of Mercy

Some of the spiritual works of mercy take a bit of maturity to be able to do. God willing, we will all be able to do them some day. Based on various passages of Scripture.

To instruct the ignorant
To counsel the doubtful
To admonish sinners
To bear wrongs patiently
To forgive offences willingly
To comfort the afflicted
To pray for the living and the dead

Mercy

To which of these works of mercy are you most attracted? In writing, pray/dream a little about the mercy you would like to do.

What is one thing that needs to change so that you will be able to take the next small step in increasing your works of mercy?

May these fruits grow in you!

Which gift or fruit does your family wish would grow in you? Write it in the apple and pray for it now.

Fruits of the Holy Spirit

You can read more about the fruits of the Spirit in Galatians 5. They come as a result of our co-operation with God.

Charity, generosity, joy, gentleness, peace, faithfulness, patience, modesty, kindness, self-control, goodness, chastity

Gifts of the Holy Spirit

These gifts are given to you at Baptism and strengthened at Confirmation. While you can do much to co-operate with God regarding these, they are gifts, not characteristics you built or earned. All of our gifts are to be used for the goodness of others.

fear of the Lord
piety
knowledge
understanding
counsel
wisdom
fortitude

Seven Contrary Virtues

In 590, Pope Gregory warned the faithful against seven sins which are deadly to the life of faith. He encouraged the virtues which overcome those temptations.

humility overcomes pride
kindness overcomes envy
abstinence overcomes gluttony
chastity overcomes lust
patience overcomes anger
generosity overcomes greed
diligence overcomes laziness

Freedom from Sin

In order to live in God, we need to conform our lives to his ways. Sin is never in God's plan and never good for us. With surrender to the dwelling of his Holy Spirit within us, we can walk freely with him. Use some of these sections for your times of reflection, personal prayer, particular examen, evening examen or examination of conscience. None of us can do this on our own, not even the strongest willed person in the world. Let God work in you.

Particular Examen

In order to make progress in living closely as Jesus did, many Christians work on one specific behavior or virtue at a time. Start with one of your faults that is affecting people around you. After making progress on external faults (one by one) eventually, move toward the more inward causes of sin and virtue.

Pray for Light
Ask for courage and grace to look with the light of the Holy Spirit at a particular fault.

Look at the last 24 hours
Once a day, look through your actions to see how you have done in the area of focus - punctuality, hope, kindness to a certain person (or whatever particular vice or virtue which you are examining).

Respond to what you see
Ask for forgiveness, thank God, ask for discernment and/or make a resolution.

Next Step
After the right amount of time (days, weeks, months), switch to analyzing another vice or virtue. Ask God's guidance in this.

Try it!

Read through this particular examen and pick a specific behavior or virtue for yourself to look for in yourself.

This week's virtue or behavior:

_____

Pray through the steps and take notes as you go:

1. Pray for Light

2. Look at the last 24 hours

3. Respond to what you see

4. Next Step

Love
does not
rejoice over
wrongdoing
but rejoices
with the
truth.

-1 Corinthians 13:6

Collection of Grace

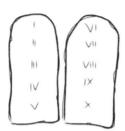

The Ten Commandments
Found in Exodus 20:1-17 and Deuteronomy 5:4-21, this marks the terms of the Covenant between God and his people. Far from being only punitive, these rules point to the essence of life.

1. I am the LORD your God:
    you shall not have strange gods before me.
2. You shall not take the name of the LORD your God in vain.
3. Remember to keep holy the LORD'S Day.
4. Honor your father and your mother.
5. You shall not kill.
6. You shall not commit adultery.
7. You shall not steal.
8. You shall not bear false witness against your neighbor.
9. You shall not covet your neighbor's wife.
10. You shall not covet your neighbor's goods.

Ten Commandments Adapted for Children
1. I am the LORD your God: don't make anything else more important than God.
2. Always use God's name with love and respect.
3. Remember to keep holy the LORD's Day by going to Mass on Sunday and making it a special day.
4. Honor your father and mother.
5. You shall not kill.
6. Be respectful to your body and other people's bodies.
7. You shall not steal.
8. You shall not lie or gossip.
9. You shall not let jealousy control your thoughts about other people's relationships.
10. You shall not let greed control your thoughts about the things people have.

Healing from Past Hurts

Sometimes our own sins can stem from a wound of ours. You may want to gently consider these things in the presence of God.

God, I wish to be free and totally yours.
Please help me to see the ways I need to be healed.
Help me to find your strength to forgive those who have hurt me.
Let me see if I have continued those wounds in my own actions.
Give me clarity if I need to make changes in my life.
Please heal me and make me free and whole.
In the name of Jesus Christ, I pray and trust.

From the Heart - Forgiveness

All throughout the Gospels, we are urged to forgive others as we have been forgiven by God. This is our path to freedom.

God, I am upset about the things that ___ has done.
Please give me the grace to forgive.
In your name, Jesus, I forgive _____ for ____.
Please bless that person.

At Home with Christ

We cannot do well on our own. Nor can we fix the sins and the bad habits in which we have become entrenched. But things are much different with Jesus. With him, there is love, security and miracles. With him, we can do the impossible.

Jesus, please take up residence in my heart.
There is so much that is broken
and I cannot fix it all myself.
I want you to be here.
Live with me and in me.
To make things right.
To make me holy.
To keep me company.
Make my heart your home.

Journal Thoughts

All of the activities on p 81 are very personal. Take time with one of these and journal about it a bit.

Addictions

What do you think are some of the most common addictions in your community?

_____

_____

_____

_____

Which of these steps brings the most hope for to you in leading a free and mentally, physically, emotionally and spiritually healthy life?

Freedom from Sinful Addictions

Sinning again and again feels devastating. 'Is it worth it to pursue closeness to God if I know I'm going to sin again?' Absolutely, yes. Through a humble heart which receives forgiveness, you are in a position to see how deeply God loves you. Jesus came to break our bondage to sin. He desires you to be free. Here's an action plan to get out of the trap:

1. Pray for God's help.
2. Analyze the times when you are tempted. What things happen right before you fall? And right before that? How can you avoid getting into the situation? Plan out a different response.
3. Discover the virtues you need which are opposite your specific addiction and the virtues you need to overcome the things that lead to sin.
4. Find the internal wound which is leading to this addiction. Talk with God about this and ask for healing. Pray to Mary.
5. Make your plan for success every morning. Renew it mid-day and in the evening. Be specific about your steps.
6. Prayerfully and privately ask for forgiveness quickly – within moments of sinning. Again, every evening.
7. Go to confession every Saturday, every two weeks or once a month. Try to find a priest who gives you good advice; then go to him consistently so he can give you even better advice, knowing your situation. Be honest. Act on the advice.
8. Find a person (friend, mentor or counselor) who can weekly or daily keep you accountable. Pray together, if possible.
9. Learn from good sources about the nature of this problem. Many other people have gone through what you are experiencing and there is a good deal of help, information and comfort.
10. Foster hope. Focus on what you love, what is good and what brings life.

Renewal of Baptismal Prayers

Our baptismal promises are usually renewed each Easter and when you attend a baptism ceremony. It can also be helpful during times of doubt, temptation or before an important event to renew them and receive strength.

Leader: Do you reject Satan?
All: I do.

Leader: And all his works?
All: I do.

Leader: And all his empty promises?
All: I do.

Leader: Do you believe in God, the Father Almighty, creator of heaven and earth?
All: I do.

Leader: Do you believe in Jesus Christ, his only Son, our Lord, who was born of the Virgin Mary was crucified, died, and was buried, rose from the dead, and is now seated at the right hand of the Father?
All: I do.

Leader: Do you believe in the Holy Spirit, the holy Catholic church, the communion of saints, the forgiveness of sins, the resurrection of the body, and life everlasting?
All: I do.

Leader: God, the all-powerful Father of our Lord Jesus Christ has given us a new birth by water and the Holy Spirit, and forgiven all our sins. May he also keep us faithful to our Lord Jesus Christ for ever and ever.

Your Profession

There may be times in life to study the creed and understand each point but in this book, the aim is to open the door to prayer- to a relationship with God. This is something dynamic and deals with how you feel / what you experience.

Which one of these baptismal promises is the most crucial at this point? Which builds your confidence and strengthens your purpose? Rewrite it here and as you do so, you are free to profess it.

Go through this examination of conscience and take notes just for yourself. This is about your own conscience, which is an inner sanctuary of a person – not to be trampled upon by others. In order to keep your notes private, just jot down a word or two which only you and God will understand. Let your word focus your prayer time on something from your life which is specific.

Inner Sanctuary

Penance and Reconciliation

Here are some tools which can help in preparing for and going to the Sacrament of Reconciliation. Frequent Confession has been one of the most instrumental sacraments in bringing me freedom.

Examination of Conscience

An examination of conscience is a good hard look at yourself. It is a time of brutal honesty and grace. Knowing that the God who created you also died to heal you of your sins, look at your actions and prepare to show him the ways you have failed so he can forgive and restore you.

Go through each of the *ten commandments (p 78)*. Have you strayed from any of these?

The *precepts of the church (p 72)* are common norms asked of all Catholics. Have you omitted any?

The *theological virtues* (p 73) of faith, hope and love are the foundation of our moral actions. Read through their description and contemplate these virtues. Have you have fallen short?

The *cardinal virtues* (p 73) are the most important qualities we can have to help us to live well. Mull over each one. How have you pursued these virtues?

The *fruits of the spirit* (p 76) come forth when we co-operate with God. Foster a desire for these fruits. Are you lacking any?

Christians are called to *works of mercy* (p 75). Are you neglecting any?

Have you fostered faith-filled attitudes? Consider the "*always attitudes*" (p 70-71). How do you need God's help?

So, you have sinned and you know it? Good! Your awareness can lead you to fall into the arms of God. Turn to Jesus. He will hold you and heal you. Do not be afraid. God loves you as you are.

Simple Preparation for the Sacrament of Reconciliation

In a calm, prayerful time, ask yourself:

- What are the things I wish I could tell God about and hear Him say, "I forgive you, completely."
- What are the things that I wish I hadn't done?
- If nothing comes to mind, don't worry. Say a quick prayer that God will help you to know yourself well and be honest. Then, ask yourself a few more questions:
- Whom have I hurt? What was it that I did that was bad?
- When have I been less than good to Jesus?
- When have I been untrue to myself?

Act of Contrition

There are many ways to make an act of contrition. At its core, it is a prayer that says, "I'm sorry."

My God, I am sorry for my sins with all my heart.
In choosing to do wrong and failing to do good,
I have sinned against you whom I love above all things.
I firmly intend, with your help, to do penance, to sin no more, and to avoid whatever leads me to sin.
Our Savior Jesus Christ suffered and died for us.
In his name, my God, have mercy.

After Confession

This is the time to do the penance that the priest mentioned. Also, you can kneel and receive God' forgiveness and mercy.

- Think about your love for Jesus and his love for you.
- Look at a crucifix and pray.
- Consider this verse: As far as the east is from the west, so far has he removed our transgressions from us. - Psalm 103:12

If you are stuck in a rut of behavior or feelings that are not good,

you
are
not
alone.

#1 After Jesus died on the cross, he descended into hell- being totally cut off from experiencing love. So – if you are feeling like you are going through hell, Jesus has literally been there too. God is with you now.

#2 Many others have done similar things as you have, but you may not realize it because it is unusual to talk about the deepest disappointments we have. Statistically speaking, it is very likely that many of your peers have gone through something similar to you.

#3 Everyone messes up. "All have sinned and fall short of the glory of God." Romans 3:23

Guilt can be good.

It shows us that our behavior does not match up to who we really are. If we feel healthy guilt, we feel that we can change.

Shame...
is not so good.

In shame, we take on the identity of sin. We think we are

Steps for the Sacrament of Penance and Reconciliation

This is the basic structure to the sacrament but some priests change it slightly to make it more like a conversation. You can bring this with you to Reconciliation if it will make it easier.

1. Make the Sign of the Cross.

2. Say "Bless me, Father, I have sinned. It has been _____ months since my last confession."

3. Priest will say something like:
"May the Lord bless you and help you to make a good confession."

4. Tell Jesus and the priest your sins.

5. Listen to advice something like:
"Very good. Try to remember that Jesus is always with you, that..."

6. Remember your Penance:
For your penance, say one "Hail Mary"
and ...Now, make your act of contrition.

7. Pray an Act of Contrition.

8. Priest absolves you of your sins:
God the Father of mercies, through the death and resurrection of your Son, you have reconciled the world to yourself ... And I absolve you of your sins, in the name of the Father, and of the Son and of the Holy Spirit. Amen.

9. Make the sign of the cross when the priest says "in the name of the Father..."

10. Leave and do your penance.

Printables at: GraceFinders.com/printable-guide-for-reconciliation/

My *Flexible* Plan

How do you want to grow? Repent? Be free? Write down the things that will help you at this season of your life. If a category does not seem to apply to you, skip it.

What actions of mine need to change and grow?

❑ Intentions, motivation:

❑ Virtues I can work on:

❑ Ways I need to be freed from sin:

❑ Times for the Sacrament of Reconciliation:

❑ Major changes I feel called to:

Dear God, I believe that you love...

The motivation I have for doing anything well is...

I really need your help to...

This chapter makes me feel...

Love,

Chapter 5

Praying with the Church

When I was little, I used to squint during the Consecration. The altar boys would ring the bells, the priest would hold up the Chalice and my eyelashes would flutter until the reflection of the gold metal danced. I stayed in that moment, knowing that something special was happening. And I felt that everyone around me was holding their breath. We all loved. We all wondered. We all celebrated. But I didn't really know anyone at my church. It almost didn't matter. I felt the same connection to the people at church when I went to Mass on one of our many road trips whether in RI, WV, CA or FL.

As I became more social my love of church increased. I went to church with friends. I became friends with the people at church. I studied scripture and started to understand why Jesus had apostles and that as his disciple, I have a role to play in the mission of the church. When I began to study the saints, my heart was in for a real shock. It became clear to me that the people I read about in books were present with me especially during the Mass. My connection to the community was not only expanding, becoming more intimate, more action oriented- it also was hopping beyond time – backwards and forwards.

What about you? How are you connected to the body of Christ? What keeps you in the heart of the church? What kind of a connection do you have?

Jesus prayed that his followers would be "one" so, prayer together is essential. In fact, since the Last Supper, Christians have been gathering for Mass. The Body of Christ is a family rich in love, kindness, and miracles. With these prayers and liturgies, you can unite yourself to God's people all around the world and with people backwards and forwards in time. Your family wants you!

Global Church

List 10 countries

List 10 states

There are people in all the places you listed who are praying for you today. Whether through the Mass, the liturgy of the hours or personal prayer, the prayer of the Church goes on and on. You are part of it! Pray now for one of the places you listed.

The Lord's Prayer...

"translated"

Our Father, who art in heaven,
God, you are our father. You are in heaven.
hallowed be thy name.
Your name is holy – it is special. Whenever we say your name, we say it with love and lots of respect.
Thy kingdom come, thy will be done,
Whatever *you* want is what *we* want. You are the one in charge.
on earth, as it is in heaven.
We want to live now just like it is in heaven.
Give us this day our daily bread,
Please give us whatever we really need today.
and forgive us our trespasses,
Please forgive us for the wrong things we've done- (forgive our sins),
as we forgive those who trespass against us.
I forgive people for bad things they have done to me.
Lead us not into temptation
Help us get out of situations where we will find it really, really hard to do the right thing.
but deliver us from evil
and save us from evil.
Amen.
I believe!

Common Catholic Prayers

The Sign of the Cross
We place ourselves in the midst of the Trinity when we pray this prayer. This reminds us of who we are since we share God's image.

In the name of the Father,
and of the Son,
and of the Holy Spirit.

Our Father
This is also called the Lord's Prayer since Jesus taught it to his disciples when they asked him how to pray. Even though most people learn it when they are very little, you can have new insights from it for life.

Our Father who art in Heaven,
hallowed be Thy Name.
Thy kingdom come,
Thy will be done on earth as it is in Heaven.
Give us this day our daily bread,
and forgive us our trespasses,
as we forgive those who trespass against us.
And lead us not into temptation,
but deliver us from evil.

Hail Mary
The first half of this prayer is what the angel Gabriel said to Mary when she was asked to be the Mother of Jesus. The second part of this prayer is our own request that Mary pray for us.

Hail Mary full of grace, the Lord is with thee.
Blessed art thou among women,
and blessed is the fruit of thy womb, Jesus.
Holy Mary, Mother of God,
pray for us sinners,
now and at the hour of our death.

Glory Be

There are two popular versions of this prayer. The first is more popular and says "world without end" which is confusing sometimes. It means that God's world - his kingdom - will never end. The second is used during the Liturgy of the Hours.

Glory Be to the Father, and to the Son, and to the Holy Spirit.
As it was in the beginning, is now, and ever shall be,
world without end.

Glory to the Father, and to the Son, and to the Holy Spirit:
as it was in the beginning, is now, and will be forever.

Memorare

"Memorare" is Latin for "Remember." Many still pray this the way their great grandparents did, using "thees" and "thous." You can certainly translate it to "you" and "your."

Remember, O most gracious Virgin Mary,
that never was it known that anyone who fled to thy protection,
implored thy help, or sought thine intercession was left unaided.
Inspired by this confidence, I fly unto thee,
O Virgin of virgins, my mother;
to thee do I come,
before thee I stand, sinful and sorrowful.
O Mother of the Word Incarnate,
despise not my petitions,
but in thy mercy hear and answer me.

Prayer to St. Michael the Archangel

Many people use this prayer to ask for protection.

St. Michael the Archangel, defend us in battle. Be our defense against the wickedness and snares of the Devil.
May God rebuke him, we humbly pray,
and do thou, O Prince of the heavenly hosts,
by the power of God,
cast into hell Satan, and all the evil spirits,
who prowl about the world
seeking the ruin of souls.

Glory Be
to the
Father,
and to the
Son,
and to the
Holy Spirit

And now these three remain: faith, hope and love. But the greatest of these is love.

As you draw your path on the labyrinth at Chartres, pray for faith, hope and love.

Collection of Grace

Act of Faith

In this theological virtue of faith, comes freedom and confidence.

O my God, I firmly believe
that you are one God in three divine Persons,
Father, Son, and Holy Spirit.
I believe that your divine Son became man
and died for our sins and that he will come
to judge the living and the dead.
I believe these and all the truths
which the Holy Catholic Church teaches
because you have revealed them
who are eternal truth and wisdom,
who can neither deceive nor be deceived.
In this faith I intend to live and die.

Act of Hope

Ultimately all our hope is in God's redemption of that which we love.

O Lord God,
I hope by your grace for the pardon
of all my sins
and after life here to gain eternal happiness
because you have promised it
who are infinitely powerful, faithful, kind,
and merciful.
In this hope I intend to live and die.

Act of Love

Making a prayerful act of love can translate into power for living with love.

O Lord God, I love you above all things,
and I love my neighbor for your sake
because you are the highest, infinite and perfect
good, worthy of all my love.
In this love I intend to live and die.

Prayers for the Faithful Departed

Since we are united as the body of Christ, our love and prayers help everyone – even those who have died.

Eternal rest grant unto them, O Lord,
and let perpetual light shine upon them.
May the souls of all the faithful departed,
through the mercy of God, rest in peace.

Guardian Angel Prayer

It is good to remember that God has given angels to protect us.

Angel of God, my guardian dear,
To whom God's love commits me here,
Ever this day, be at my side,
To light and guard, rule and guide.

Prayer to the Holy Spirit

This can be prayed any time, but it is particularly popular around Pentecost.

Come Holy Spirit, fill the hearts of your faithful
and kindle in them the fire of your love.
Send forth your Spirit
and they shall be created.
And You shall renew the face of the earth.

O, God, who by the light of the Holy Spirit,
did instruct the hearts of the faithful,
grant that by the same Holy Spirit
we may be truly wise and ever enjoy His consolations,
Through Christ Our Lord.

Holy Water Font

A holy water is at a church door is to remind you of your baptism.

In the name of the Father, and of the Son and of the Holy Spirit.
Thank you, God for saving me. I recommit to your mission, given to me at baptism.

For such a time as this

When might you pray these prayers? Describe the occasion and how you would initiate it.

Prayers for the Faithful Departed:

Guardian Angel Prayer:

Prayer to the Holy Spirit:

Holy Water Font:

These have a wonderful rhythm and impart wisdom time after time as they are prayed and practiced.

Who is someone you can pray this with?

List his or her name above.
If the person is nearby, try it now.
Otherwise, commit to a certain time and day.

Collection of Grace

The Angelus

This prayer is said at noon and 6pm at St. Peter's Basilica, joined by Christians all around the world.

Leader: The Angel of the Lord declared to Mary:
All:　and she conceived of the Holy Spirit. *Hail Mary...*

Leader: Behold the handmaid of the Lord:
All:　be it done unto me according to Thy word. *Hail Mary...*

Leader: And the Word was made Flesh:
All:　and dwelt among us. *Hail Mary...*

Leader: Pray for us, O Holy Mother of God:
All:　that we may be made worthy of the promises of Christ.

Let us pray:
Pour forth, we beseech Thee, O Lord, Thy grace into our hearts; that we, to whom the incarnation of Christ, Thy Son, was made known by the message of an angel, may by His Passion and Cross be brought to the glory of His Resurrection, through the same Christ Our Lord.

Regina Coeli

During Eastertime, this prayer is said instead of the Angelus.

Leader: Queen of Heaven, rejoice, alleluia. /
All:　For He whom you did merit to bear, alleluia.

Leader: Has risen, as he said, alleluia. /
All:　Pray for us to God, alleluia.

Leader: Rejoice and be glad, O Virgin Mary, alleluia. /
All:　For the Lord has truly risen, alleluia.

Let us pray:
O God, who gave joy to the world through the resurrection of Thy Son, our Lord Jesus Christ, grant we beseech Thee, that through the intercession of the Virgin Mary, His Mother, we may obtain the joys of everlasting life. Through the same Christ our Lord.

Mass Prayers

You can use this as a guide during Mass or use these prayers throughout your day. It can help children to know and understand what they are experiencing. Some of the parts may be a little different during Mass since the priest has a few options of prayers to choose from and I have only listed the most common.

Introductory Rite
In the name of the Father, and of the Son, and of the Holy Spirit. Amen.

The grace of our Lord Jesus Christ, and the love of God, and the communion of the Holy Spirit be with you all.
…And with your spirit.

Penitential Act
Near the beginning of Mass, we acknowledge our sins, as if to get this out in the open quickly, so that we may proceed honestly and face to face with the Lord.

I confess to almighty God
and to you, my brothers and sisters,
that I have greatly sinned,
in my thoughts and in my words,
in what I have done and in what I have failed to do,

(striking the breast)
through my fault, through my fault,
through my most grievous fault;
therefore I ask blessed Mary ever-Virgin,
all the Angels and Saints,
and you, my brothers and sisters,
to pray for me to the Lord our God.

Kyrie Eleison
One of the only prayers sometimes said in Greek, during the Mass.

Lord have mercy.
Christ have mercy.
Lord have mercy.

You can bring this book to Mass and use this portion to participate more fully. It is much easier if you know what you are saying! Perhaps less embarrassing would be using this along with a streaming Mass online. At anytime of day, there is probably a Mass in English being streamed. Check out:

Mass-online.com

https://mass-online.org/daily-holy-mass-live-online/

Look up a Mass that is going on presently. Where is that Mass?

_____

What is a weekday and time that you could pray with an online Mass? (circle one)

Mon Tue Wed Thu Fri

What time?

This is meant to be a triumphant prayer. Which part of this is most joyful for you? Draw an arrow.

triumphant

Collection of Grace

Gloria

During the subdued days of Lent, we do not pray this at Mass which makes it all the more dynamic during Easter. It makes a great morning prayer.

Glory to God in the highest, and on earth peace to people of good will.
We praise you,
we bless you,
we adore you,
we glorify you,
we give you thanks for your great glory,
Lord God, heavenly King,
O God, almighty Father.
Lord Jesus Christ, Only Begotten Son,
Lord God, Lamb of God, Son of the Father,
you take away the sins of the world,
have mercy on us;
you take away the sins of the world,
receive our prayer;
you are seated at the right hand of the Father,
have mercy on us.
For you alone are the Holy One,
you alone are the Lord,
you alone are the Most High, Jesus Christ,
with the Holy Spirit,
in the glory of God the Father.

Liturgy of the Word
The Word of the Lord …Thanks be to God.

The Lord be with you …and with your spirit

A reading from the holy Gospel according to N.
(Trace a little cross on your forehead, lips and chest.)
…Glory to you, O Lord.

The Gospel of the Lord.
…Praise to you, Lord Jesus Christ.

96

The Nicene Creed

This profession of faith is held in common with Catholics, all eastern churches and most Protestant churches.

I believe in one God, the Father almighty,
maker of heaven and earth,
of all things visible and invisible.

I believe in one Lord Jesus Christ,
the Only Begotten Son of God,
born of the Father before all ages.
God from God, Light from Light,
true God from true God,
begotten, not made, consubstantial with the Father;
through him all things were made.

For us men and for our salvation
he came down from heaven,
and by the Holy Spirit was incarnate of the Virgin Mary,
and became man. *(bow your head)*

For our sake he was crucified under Pontius Pilate,
he suffered death and was buried,
and rose again on the third day
in accordance with the Scriptures.

He ascended into heaven
and is seated at the right hand of the Father.
He will come again in glory
to judge the living and the dead
and his kingdom will have no end.

I believe in the Holy Spirit, the Lord, the giver of life,
who proceeds from the Father and the Son,
who with the Father and the Son is adored and glorified,
who has spoken through the prophets.

I believe in one, holy, catholic and apostolic Church.
I confess one Baptism for the forgiveness of sins
and I look forward to the resurrection of the dead
and the life of the world to come.

All are welcome to profess this belief.

unity of the church

Pope John Paul II was dedicated to the unity of all Christians. He said,

"Believers in Christ, united in following in the footsteps of the martyrs, cannot remain divided...they must profess together the same truth about the Cross."
— Ut Unum Sint

Pray now for the unity of the church. Who do you know of various parts, denominations and factions of the Christian church? Jot some of their names in the heart.

Bring love to your prayer for these people and all brothers and sisters- that we would be united.

Collection of Grace

The Apostles' Creed

Early Christians stated the basic parts of their belief in Jesus and they memorized these articles of faith. The Apostles' Creed is sometimes professed during Mass (mostly used during Easter.)

I believe in God,
the Father almighty,
Creator of heaven and earth,
and in Jesus Christ, his only Son, our Lord,
who was conceived by the Holy Spirit,
born of the Virgin Mary,
suffered under Pontius Pilate,
was crucified, died and was buried;
he descended into hell;
on the third day he rose again from the dead;
he ascended into heaven,
and is seated at the right hand of God the Father almighty;
from there he will come to judge the living and the dead.

I believe in the Holy Spirit,
the holy catholic Church,
the communion of saints,
the forgiveness of sins,
the resurrection of the body,
and life everlasting.

Preparation of the Gifts
When the basket is passed for the collection, I always think about placing all my work from the past week into it. It goes to the foot of the altar.

Blessed are you, Lord God of all creation,
for through your goodness we have received the bread we offer
you: fruit of the earth and work of human hands, it will become for
us the bread of life.
…Blessed be God for ever.

[By the mystery of this water and wine may we come to share in
the divinity of Christ, who humbled himself to share in our
humanity] Blessed are you, Lord God of all creation, for through
your goodness we have received the wine we offer you:
fruit of the vine and work of human hands, it will become our
spiritual drink.
…Blessed be God for ever.

[Lord God, we ask you to receive us and be pleased with the
sacrifice we offer you with humble and contrite hearts. // Lord,
wash away my iniquity; cleanse me from my sin].

All stand up
*In our own personal prayer, we could repeat these words that the
priest whispers as he bows.*

With humble spirit and contrite heart
may we be accepted by you, O Lord,
and may our sacrifice in your sight this day
be pleasing to you, Lord God.

Orate, Fratres
Pray, brothers and sisters, that my sacrifice and yours may be
acceptable to God, the almighty Father.
…May the Lord accept the sacrifice at your hands
for the praise and glory of his name, for our good
and the good of all his holy Church.

"through your goodness we have **received.**"

Dwell on this line from the preparation of the gifts. What have you received? List as many things as you can fit in this space. As you write or type, let each word formation be a prayer of gratitude.

Anamnesis

Etym. Greek *anamnesis*, calling to mind, recollection

Remember

During the Liturgy of the Eucharist, we call to mind the Lord's passion, death, resurrection and ascension in such a way that it becomes present.

Spend a little time thinking about the events of Jesus' life. Let them become present to you.

Next time you go to Mass, unite this feeling and prayer with the whole community – and the history of the Holy Spirit's work on earth. It is an understatement that a lot is being brought to you.

Collection of Grace

Eucharistic Prayer
The Lord be with you.
…And with your spirit.

Lift up your hearts.
…We lift them up to the Lord.

Let us give thanks to the Lord our God.
…It is right and just.

Sanctus
We join the angels and saints in praising God as we repeat the words that Isaiah heard in a vision of heaven.

Holy, Holy, Holy Lord God of hosts.
Heaven and earth are full of your glory.
Hosanna in the highest.
Blessed is he who comes in the name of the Lord.
Hosanna in the highest.

(All kneel)

Memorial Acclamations
We proclaim your Death, O Lord, and profess your Resurrection, until you come again.
  or
When we eat this Bread and drink this Cup, we proclaim your Death, O Lord, until you come again.
  or
Save us, Saviour of the world, for by your Cross and Resurrection you have set us free.

(All stand up)

The Lord's Prayer

Our Father, who art in heaven, hallowed be thy name...

After the Lord's prayer, this embolism is what the priest prays.

Deliver us, Lord, we pray, from every evil,
graciously grant peace in our days,
that, by the help of your mercy,
we may be always free from sin
and safe from all distress,
as we await the blessed hope
and the coming of our Savior, Jesus Christ.

...For the kingdom, the power and the glory are yours now and
forever.

Sign of Peace

Lord Jesus Christ, who said to your Apostles:
Peace I leave you, my peace I give you;
look not on our sins, but on the faith of your Church,
and graciously grant her peace and unity
in accordance with your will.
Who live and reign forever and ever.
...Amen.

(All stand up)

The peace of the Lord be with you always.
...And with your spirit.

Let us offer each other a sign of peace.
...peace be with you.

Sign of Peace

List ways you indicate peace. As
you write, pray with peace for these
people.

1. To a stranger

2. To someone you live with

3. To someone older than you

4. To a friend

5. In your family

Crossword Puzzle

1. Unity

2. To walk up as in a formal line

3. Respectfully and with intention

4. Serious

5. To get something

6. In the state of grace

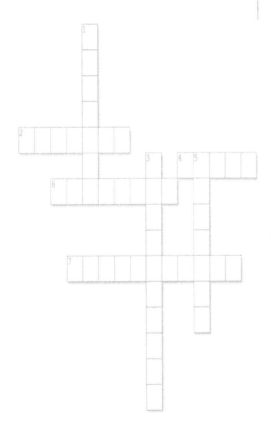

Collection of Grace

Lamb of God

Sometimes this is called by its Latin words, "Agnus Dei."

Lamb of God,
you take away the sins of the world,
have mercy on us.
Lamb of God,
you take away the sins of the world,
have mercy on us.
Lamb of God,
you take away the sins of the world,
grant us peace.

Behold the Lamb of God,
behold him who takes away the sins of the world.
Blessed are those called to the supper of the Lamb.

…Lord, I am not worthy that you should enter under my roof,
but only say the word and my soul shall be healed.

(All kneel)

Holy Communion

In order to be properly disposed to receive Communion, participants should not be conscious of grave sin and normally should have fasted for one hour.

Because Catholics believe that the celebration of the Eucharist is a sign of the reality of the oneness of faith, life, and worship, members of those churches with whom we are not yet fully united are ordinarily not admitted to Holy Communion… We pray that our common baptism and the action of the Holy Spirit in this Eucharist will draw us closer to one another and begin to dispel the sad divisions which separate us. We pray that these will lessen and finally disappear, in keeping with Christ's prayer for us "that they may all be one" (Jn 17:21). – adapted slightly from the USCCB

Those receiving process up with one hand under the other, reverently receive the body of Christ. Those not receiving can celebrate and participate through prayer and singing in the pew.

The body of Christ
…Amen

Spiritual Communion

If you would like to go to daily Mass more often but you cannot, this is a very powerful prayer for you. It is good also, if you are infirmed or isolated in a situation where it is not possible to get to Mass, or for those who should not receive the Eucharist because of sin or those who have broken their fast. You could also say a prayer like this from the heart.

My Jesus, I believe that You are present
in the Most Holy Sacrament.
I love You above all things,
and I desire to receive You into my soul.
Since I cannot at this moment receive You sacramentally,
come at least spiritually into my heart.
I embrace You as if You were already there
and unite myself wholly to You.
Never permit me to be separated from You.

Conclusion
The Lord be with you.
…And with your spirit.

Blessing
May almighty God bless you,
the Father, (+) and the Son and
the Holy Spirit.
…Amen.

Dismissal
Go forth, the Mass is ended.
   or
Go and announce the Gospel of the Lord.
   or
Go in peace, glorifying the Lord by your life.
   or
Go in peace.
…Thanks be to God.

Blessing and Command

This blessing at the end is part of the climax of the Mass. To an Israelite, the blessing of the father was sought after – it was a special delivery of goodness, riches and power. The father gives what is his to his son. Likewise, at this point in the Mass, through the priest, God gives you goodness, riches and power through his son.

Notice there is a command right after this blessing…

Which of these commands to go means the most action for you? Draw an arrow.

Pause for a moment after receiving the Eucharist or after making a Spiritual Communion (p 103) to dwell with Our Lord.

Prayer does not need any words.

It can just be **presence**. Your presence to God and God's presence to you.

an embrace
a stillness
a look
just being
the power of life

Try it now.

Thanksgiving After Mass

Since we are so closely united to Jesus after Communion, try taking a moment after Mass to speak intimately to him with this prayer from St. Thomas Aquinas.

Lord, Father all-powerful and ever-living God, I thank You, for even though I am a sinner, your unprofitable servant, not because of my worth but in the kindness of your mercy, You have fed me with the Precious Body and Blood of Your Son, our Lord Jesus Christ.

I pray that this Holy Communion may not bring me condemnation and punishment but forgiveness and salvation.
May it be a helmet of faith and a shield of good will.
May it purify me from evil ways
and put an end to my evil passions.
May it bring me charity and patience, humility and obedience,
and growth in the power to do good.

May it be my strong defense against all my enemies,
visible and invisible,
and the perfect calming of all my evil impulses,
bodily and spiritual.

May it unite me more closely to you, the One true God,
and lead me safely through death to everlasting happiness with You.

And I pray that You will lead me, a sinner,
to the banquet where you,
with Your Son and Holy Spirit, are true and perfect light,
total fulfillment, everlasting joy, gladness without end,
and perfect happiness to your saints.
Grant this through Christ our Lord.

Chaplets and Litanies

The Chaplet of Divine Mercy

This set of prayers was given in prayer to St. Faustina. It is prayed on the Rosary beads. The painting with the words,
"Jesus, I trust in you" is the Divine Mercy image.

Opening Prayer
You expired, Jesus, but the source of life gushed forth for souls,
and the ocean of mercy opened up for the whole world.
O Fount of Life, unfathomable Divine Mercy,
envelop the whole world and empty Yourself out upon us.

(Repeat three times)
O Blood and Water, which gushed forth from the Heart of Jesus
as a fount of mercy for us, I trust in You!

The first 3 beads: Our Father, Hail Mary and the Apostle's Creed

On the first isolated bead of each decade, pray:
Eternal Father, I offer you the Body and Blood, Soul and Divinity
of Your Dearly Beloved Son, Our Lord, Jesus Christ,
in atonement for our sins and those of the whole world.

On each of the 10 "Hail Mary" beads, pray:
For the sake of His sorrowful Passion,
have mercy on us and on the whole world.

Concluding prayer (Repeat 3 times)
Holy God, Holy Mighty One, Holy Immortal One,
have mercy on us and on the whole world.

Closing Prayer
Eternal God, in whom mercy is endless and the treasury of
compassion inexhaustible, look kindly upon us and increase Your
mercy in us, that in difficult moments we might not despair nor
become despondent, but with great confidence submit ourselves to
Your holy will, which is Love and Mercy itself.

Try it!

The Chaplet of Divine Mercy takes about 15 minutes. Follow the directions and try it now. Who will you offer this prayer for?

- ❑ Personal
- ❑ Family
- ❑ Friend
- ❑ Community
- ❑ Nation
- ❑ Poor
- ❑ Global

Follow the directions in italics and read the prayers.

After having prayed this, what questions do you have? Is it confusing? Can you do this prayer on your own?

Listen to the Tantum Ergo

You can try these versions on YouTube or search for others:
https://youtu.be/Swns4Kjzc9E
or https://youtu.be/ExNIxKsGTn8

Notice the **tone** and the **feeling** conveyed. Use three adjectives to convey it.

-
-
-

Have you ever gone to a church where the Eucharist was on display (exposed) for prayer and adoration? These two prayers on the right are often said just before the Eucharist is brought back to the tabernacle (at the end of the public prayer). If you can attend this, I highly recommend you do. Alternatively, you can find places around the world who are livestreaming Adoration.
https://www.ewtn.com/catholicism/adoration

Whether in a church, live stream or just quietly wherever you are, spend three minutes in Adoration. See if you can convey the three adjectives that you listed above.

Were you able to?

❏ Yes   ❏ No   ❏ Sort of

Benediction - Tantum Ergo

This is sometimes prayed during Eucharistic Adoration when a priest or deacon is leading worship. It is by St. Thomas Aquinas.

Tantum ergo Sacramentum	(So great therefore a sacrament)
veneremur cernui	(let us venerate with bowed heads)
et antiquum documentum	(and the ancient document)
novo cedat ritui	(to the new, give way,)
Praestet fides supplementum	(may supply faith a supplement)
Sensuum defectui.	(for the defect of the senses)
Genitori Genitoque	(To the One who generates and to the one who is generated)
Laus et jubilatio	(be praise and joy)
Salus, honor, virtus, quoque	(health, honor, strength also)
sit et benedictio	(may there be and blessing)
Procedenti ab utroque	(to the One proceeding from both)
Compar sit laudatio	(equal may there be praise)

The Divine Praises

This is usually prayed after Benediction during Eucharistic adoration, just before the Host is returned to the Tabernacle.

Blessed be God.
Blessed be His Holy Name.
Blessed be Jesus Christ, true God and true Man.
Blessed be the Name of Jesus.
Blessed be His Most Sacred Heart.
Blessed be His Most Precious Blood.
Blessed be Jesus in the Most Holy Sacrament of the Altar.
Blessed be the Holy Spirit, the Paraclete.
Blessed be the great Mother of God, Mary most Holy.
Blessed be her Holy and Immaculate Conception.
Blessed be her Glorious Assumption.
Blessed be the name of Mary, Virgin and Mother.
Blessed be St. Joseph, her most chaste spouse.
Blessed be God in His Angels and in His Saints. Amen.

May the heart of Jesus, in the Most Blessed Sacrament, be praised, adored, and loved with grateful affection, at every moment, in all the tabernacles of the world, even to the end of time.

Stations of the Cross

Catholics often pray the stations of the cross (via dolorosa) at Church on Fridays in Lent. The stations are posted on the walls along the nave. After announcing each station, you can say a prayer which contemplates that action of the Lord. Then say:

Leader: We Adore you, O Christ,
and we praise you...
(all genuflect)

All: ...because by your Holy Cross,
you have redeemed the world.
(all make the sign of the cross)

The first station - Jesus is condemned to death
Oh, God, thank you for bearing my own condemnation. Please help me to live for you.

The second station - Jesus carries His cross
Jesus, I can barely carry my own cross in life. I will take courage from your loving example.

The third station - Jesus falls the first time
I am sorry that my sins caused you so much pain. When I fall, help me to get up and follow you again.

The fourth station - Jesus meets his mother
Mary, your confidence in the midst of sorrow must have been strong. Teach me to have faith and to support those around me like you do.

The fifth station - Simon of Cyrene helps Jesus to carry his cross
There are so many people who help me through life, as Simon helped you. Let me be a willing servant to those in need.

The sixth station - Veronica wipes the face of Jesus
When Veronica reached out with compassion, your imprint was left on her cloth. I recognize that you leave your imprint on my heart when I encounter you in the suffering.

Which station is your favorite?

Try to BE PRESENT at the scene. What do you notice?

Noticing

As you contemplate the stations of the cross, notice:

- ❑ Jesus' humility
- ❑ A moment of grace for you
- ❑ Courage that it creates

Which stations evoke these points for you? Write about it.

Collection of Grace

The seventh station - Jesus falls the second time
Again, Lord, you stumble. How often I return to bad habits and sin again and again. Lord, help me in my weakness.

The eighth station - Jesus meets the women of Jerusalem
Thank you, God for the good people who love you and who support me when I am in great need. Let me be one of those people too.

The ninth station - Jesus falls a third time
It saddens my heart to contemplate the extreme personal suffering you went through. Do you still suffer, Lord, when we are in pain?

The tenth station - Jesus clothes are taken away
You know what it is like to have your dignity stripped from you. And yet, still, you must have known you were loved. Help us too, Lord, to find our identity in God, our Father.

The eleventh station - Jesus is nailed to the cross
It is too much to take in- that you were nailed to a cross for my sins. How did you choose this?

The twelfth station - Jesus dies on the cross
As I contemplate your death, I remember all who have died. May your death mean life for them.

The thirteenth station - Jesus is taken down from the cross
Did your friends and family feel defeated? How could they have guessed the immense grace that was coming from this act of love.

The fourteenth station - Jesus is laid in the tomb
The tomb seems so final- so lifeless but you knew the end as you walked this path. Help me to trust.

Litany of Trust

This prayer was written by the Sisters of Life (sistersoflife.org) They do a lot of work with mothers in difficult situations.

That You are continually holding me,
sustaining me, loving me   *Jesus, I trust in You.*

That Your love goes deeper than my
sins and failings, and transforms me   *Jesus, I trust in You.*

That not knowing what tomorrow
brings is an invitation to lean on You   *Jesus, I trust in You.*

That You are with me in my suffering   *Jesus, I trust in You.*

That my suffering, united to Your own,
will bear fruit in this life and the next   *Jesus, I trust in You.*

That You will not leave me orphan,
that You are present in Your Church   *Jesus, I trust in You.*

That Your plan is better
than anything else   *Jesus, I trust in You.*

That You always hear me and in
Your goodness always respond to me   *Jesus, I trust in You.*

That You give me the grace to accept
forgiveness and to forgive others   *Jesus, I trust in You.*

That You give me all the strength
I need for what is asked   *Jesus, I trust in You.*

That my life is a gift   *Jesus, I trust in You.*

That You will teach me to trust You   *Jesus, I trust in You.*

That You are my Lord and my God   *Jesus, I trust in You.*

That I am Your beloved one   *Jesus, I trust in You.*

Draw an arrow to the statement that **you most need** to pray this week.

Jesus, I trust in You.

Can you pray this with your breath? (see aspiration prayers on p. 30)

☐ Yes   ☐ No   ☐ Sort of

109

Write your own litany of humility

that would be more appropriate for you and your friends.

From the desire of being

_____

from the fear of _____

That_____ Jesus,
grant me the grace to desire it.

That others _____

and I _____.

Litany of Humility

A lot of people have a hard time wanting to pray this prayer the first few times they see it. However, those who pray it, experience much freedom.

O Jesus! meek and humble of heart, hear me.
From the desire of being esteemed,

...deliver me, Jesus.

From the desire of being loved...
From the desire of being extolled ...
From the desire of being honored ...
From the desire of being praised ...
From the desire of being preferred to others...
From the desire of being consulted ...
From the desire of being approved ...
From the fear of being humiliated ...
From the fear of being despised...
From the fear of suffering rebukes ...
From the fear of being calumniated ...
From the fear of being forgotten ...
From the fear of being ridiculed ...
From the fear of being wronged ...
From the fear of being suspected ...

That others may be loved more than I,

...Jesus, grant me the grace to desire it.

That others may be esteemed more than I ...
That, in the opinion of the world,
others may increase and I may decrease ...
That others may be chosen and I set aside ...
That others may be praised and I unnoticed ...
That others may be preferred to me in everything...
That others may become holier than I, provided that I may become as holy as I should…

Litany of the Saints

It is almost impossible for me to hear the Litany of the Saints at church and not cry. I feel a strong connection to the Christians who have gone before us and who are cheering us on in the battle. You can make your own litany of the saints by saying the name of a saint and then respond, pray for us. When praying with others, you can alternate who calls out a saint name.

Holy Mary,
pray for us
(repeat after each line)
Holy Mother of God,
Holy Virgin of virgins,
St. Michael,
St. Gabriel,
St. Raphael,
All you holy angels and archangels,
All you holy orders of blessed spirits,
St. John the Baptist,
St. Joseph,
All you holy patriarchs and prophets,
St. Peter,
St. Paul,
St. Andrew,
St. James,
St. John,
St. Thomas,
St. James,
St. Philip,
St. Bartholomew,
St. Matthew,

St. Simon,
St. Thaddeus,
St. Matthias,
St. Barnabas,
St. Luke,
St. Mark,
All you holy apostles and evangelists,
All you holy disciples of our Lord,
All you holy innocents,
St. Stephen,
St. Lawrence,
St. Vincent,
SS. Fabian and Sebastian,
St. John and Paul,
St. Cosmas and Damian,
St. Gervase and Protase,
All you holy Martyrs,
St. Sylvester,
St. Gregory,
St. Ambrose,
St. Augustine,
St. Jerome,

St. Martin,
St. Nicholas,
All you holy bishops and confessors,
All you holy doctors,
St. Anthony,
St. Benedict,
St. Bernard,
St. Dominic,
St. Francis,
All you holy priests and Levites,
All you holy monks and hermits,
St. Mary Magdalen,
St. Agatha,
St. Lucy,
St. Agnes,
St. Cecilia,
St. Catherine,
St. Anastasia,
All you holy virgins and widows,
All you holy men and women, saints of God, intercede for us.

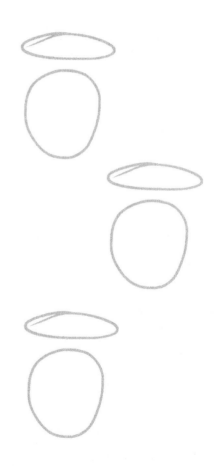

Who are your favorite Saints?

If you do not know any, look up 3 from this list on
https://www.catholic.org/saints/stindex.php

Write their names in the halos.

Praying the Rosary is a way of

contemplating the lives of Jesus and Mary

The important part is to

think about

the mysteries

– less mental attention goes to saying the words of the prayers. This can be very tricky for some people. How is it for you?

It can help to look at an image of the mystery you are praying.

Rosary Resources

The Rosary is a form of meditation but also is very helpful in petitioning for the needs of friends, family and the world. Use the resources here to make it part of your life.

The Mysteries of the Rosary

The Joyful Mysteries
1. The Annunciation
2. The Visitation
3. The Nativity
4. The Presentation of Jesus at the temple
5. The Finding of Jesus in the temple

The Luminous Mysteries
1. The Baptism of the Lord
2. The Wedding at Cana
3. The Proclamation of the Kingdom
4. The Transfiguration
5. The Institution of the Eucharist

The Sorrowful Mysteries
1. Agony in the garden at Gethsemane
2. Scourging of Jesus at the pillar
3. Crowning with thorns
4. Carrying of the Cross
5. The Crucifixion

The Glorious Mysteries
1. The Resurrection
2. The Ascension of Jesus
3. The Descent of the Holy Spirit at Pentecost
4. The Assumption of Mary
5. The Coronation of Mary as Queen of Heaven

Mysteries for Each Day of the Week

Choose which set of Mysteries you will pray. You can choose any mystery on any day but this is the order traditionally practiced around the world:

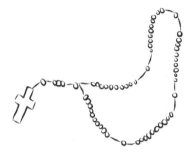

Sunday-   Glorious
Monday-   Joyful
Tuesday-   Sorrowful
Wednesday-   Glorious
Thursday-   Luminous
Friday-   Sorrowful
Saturday-   Joyful

How to Pray the Rosary

Pray the first segment of three beads

Sign of the Cross	– hold the cross
Apostle's Creed	– solitary bead
Our Father (for the intentions of the Pope)	– solitary bead
Hail Mary (for an increase in faith)	– 1st little bead
Hail Mary (for an increase in hope)	– 2nd little bead
Hail Mary (for an increase in love)	– 3rd little bead
Glory Be	– solitary bead
Fatima Prayer	– solitary bead

Pray each decade

Announce the name and number of the mystery.	
Read Scripture about that mystery (optional)	– solitary bead
Offer this mystery for an intention (optional)	– solitary bead
Our Father	– solitary bead
10 Hail Marys (optional scripture before each)	– ten beads
Glory Be	– solitary bead
Fatima Prayer	– solitary bead
Repeat this for all 5 mysteries.	

Pray the middle clasp/bead
Hail Holy Queen
Finish with the sign of the cross

What are **your impressions** about the Rosary (from childhood, school, media, family)? Check all that apply.

- ❑ Super holy
- ❑ Old people
- ❑ Mean
- ❑ Good
- ❑ Powerful
- ❑ Confusing
- ❑ Feminine
- ❑ Mysterious
- ❑ Peaceful
- ❑ Selfless
- ❑ Helpful
- ❑ Boring
- ❑ Others:

Ask God if these impressions will help or hinder you. Are there new impressions would God like to show you for this stage of your life? Muse about these things with God and jot a few notes in the thought bubble.

life is full

But there is **always room for God** in the same way that there is always time enough to breath. Where / when can you pray one of the chaplets, rosary or litanies *regularly* into your life – in a way that fits well?

- ❏ During a commute
- ❏ After lunch
- ❏ Waiting for something to begin
- ❏ Before bed
- ❏ When I can't fall asleep at night
- ❏ Right after work/school
- ❏ While walking
- ❏ While doing mindless chores
- ❏ Other ideas:

Prayers Unique to the Rosary

Fatima Prayer
This was told by Mary in an apparition to three children in Fatima, Portugal in 1917.
O my Jesus forgive us our sins, save us from the fires of Hell; lead all souls to Heaven, especially those in most need of Thy mercy.

Hail Holy Queen
Hail, Holy Queen, Mother of mercy, our life, our sweetness and our hope. To thee do we cry, poor banished children of Eve. To thee do we send up our sighs, mourning and weeping in this valley of tears. Turn, then, most gracious advocate, thine eyes of mercy toward us, and after this, our exile, show unto us the blessed fruit of thy womb, Jesus. O clement, O loving, O sweet Virgin Mary.

V. Pray for us, O holy Mother of God.
R. That we may be made worthy of the promises of Christ.

The following is added after the "Hail, Holy Queen":
Let us pray. O God, Whose Only-Begotten Son, by His life, death and resurrection, has purchased for us the rewards of eternal life: grant, we beseech Thee, that by meditating upon these mysteries of the most holy Rosary of the Blessed Virgin Mary, we may imitate what they contain, and obtain what they promise, through the same Christ our Lord. Amen.

Rosary Adaptations
If praying the Rosary is difficult at times, here are some adaptions:

- Pray one decade per day.
- With a family, only do as many Hail Marys in a decade for each person to lead one.
- Sing Ave Maria in place of the decade of Hail Marys (while meditating on mysteries).
- Pray a "one handed" rosary – only 5 Hail Marys per decade.
- Pray along with an audio app.
- Do a Rosary walk and pray one mystery per block.

A Scriptural Rosary

If you would like Scripture to help you meditate on the mysteries, you can take one verse for each Hail Mary bead. Read it first then pray the Hail Mary. Or, you can read a few verses at the start of the decade, then do all the prayers. The following verses are not "official", they are adapted from www.scripturalrosary.org. You can use others too.

The First Joyful Mystery
The Annunciation

The angel Gabriel was sent by God to a city of Galilee to a virgin betrothed to a man whose name was Joseph, of the house of David; and the Virgin's name was Mary. Lk 1:26-27

He came to her and said, "Hail, full of grace!" "The Lord is with you!" Lk 1:28

But she was greatly troubled at the saying, and considered in her mind what sort of greeting this might be. Lk 1:29

And the angel said to her, "Do not be afraid, Mary, for you have found favor with God." Lk 1:30

"And behold, you will conceive in your womb and bear a son, and you shall call his name Jesus." Lk 1:31

Mary said to the angel, "How can this be, since I have no husband?" Lk 1:34

The angel said to her, "The Holy Spirit will come upon you, and the power of the Most High will overshadow you; therefore the child to be born will be called Holy, the Son of God." Lk 1:35

And Mary said, "Behold, I am the handmaid of the Lord; let it be done to me according to your word." Lk 1:38

And the Word became flesh and dwelt among us. Jn 1:14

The Joyful Mysteries

Prayer Requests

As you pray the Rosary, you can lift up the things that you and your loved ones need. You can pray for the world. Consider listing your prayer requests.

Collection of Grace

The Second Joyful Mystery

The Visitation

In those days Mary arose and went with haste into the hill country, to a city of Judah, and she entered the house of Zechariah and greeted Elizabeth. Lk 1:39-40

And when Elizabeth heard the greeting of Mary, the babe leaped in her womb. Lk 1:41

And Elizabeth was filled with the Holy Spirit, and she exclaimed with a loud cry, "Blessed are you among women!" Lk 1:42

"And blessed is the fruit of your womb!" Lk 1:42

"And why is this granted me, that the mother of the Lord should come to me?" Lk 1:43

"For behold, when the voice of your greeting came to my ears, the babe in my womb leaped for joy." Lk 1:44

"And blessed is she who believed there would be a fulfillment of what was spoken to her from the Lord." Lk 1:45

And Mary said, "My soul magnifies the Lord." Lk 1:46

"And my spirit rejoices in God my Savior." Lk 1:47

And Mary remained with her about three months, and returned to her home. Lk 1:56

The Third Joyful Mystery

The Nativity of the Lord

When his mother Mary had been betrothed to Joseph, before they came together she was found to be with child of the Holy Spirit. Mt 1:18

And her husband Joseph, being a just man and unwilling to put her to shame, resolved to send her away quietly. Mt 1:19

Behold, an angel of the Lord appeared to him in a dream, saying, "Joseph, son of David, do not fear to take Mary your wife." Mt 1:20

"For that which is conceived in her is of the Holy Spirit." Mt 1:20

"She will bear a son, and you shall call his name Jesus, for he will save his people from their sins." Mt 1:21

When Joseph woke from sleep, he did as the angel of the Lord commanded him. Mt 1:24

Joseph went up from Galilee, from the city of Nazareth, to Judea, to the city of David, which is called Bethlehem, to be enrolled with Mary his betrothed, who was with child. Lk 2:4

While they were there the time came for her to be delivered. And she gave birth to her firstborn son. Lk 2:7

And she wrapped him in swaddling clothes, and laid him in a manger, because there was no place for them in the inn. Lk 2:7

God sent forth his son, born of woman, born under the law, to redeem those who were under the law, so that we might receive adoption as sons. Gal 4:4-5

Rosary journal

As you meditate on the mysteries of the Rosary, feel free to note any insights you have about the lives of Jesus and Mary – and/or how yours relates to theirs.

Prayer Requests

As you pray the Rosary, you can lift up the things that you and your loved ones need. You can pray for the world. Consider listing your prayer requests.

The Fourth Joyful Mystery
The Presentation

When the time came for their purification according to the law of Moses, they brought him up to Jerusalem to present him to the Lord. Lk 2:22

Now there was a man in Jerusalem whose name was Simeon… it had been revealed to him by the Holy Spirit that he should not taste death before he had seen the Lord's Christ. Lk 2:25, 26

When the parents brought in the child Jesus, to do for him according to the law, he took him up in his arms and blessed God and said, "Lord, now lettest thou thy servant depart in peace, according to thy word." Lk 2:27-29

"For mine eyes have seen thy salvation which thou hast prepared in the presence of the peoples." Lk 2:30-31

"A light for revelation to the Gentiles, and for glory to thy people Israel." Lk 2:32

And his father and mother marveled at what was said about him. Lk 2:33

Simeon blessed them and said to his mother, "Behold, this child is set for the fall and rising of many in Israel, and for a sign which is spoken against." Lk 2:34

"And a sword shall pierce through your own soul also" Lk 2:35

And there was a prophetess, Anna…And coming up that very hour, she gave thanks to God, and spoke of him to all who were awaiting the redemption of Jerusalem. Lk 2:38

When they had performed all according to the law of the Lord, they returned into Galilee, to their own city, Nazareth. Lk 2:39

The Fifth Joyful Mystery
The Finding of the Child Jesus in the Temple

Now his parents went up to Jerusalem every year at the feast of the Passover. And when he was twelve years old, they went up according to custom. Lk 2:41-42

When the feast was ended, as they were returning, the boy Jesus stayed behind in Jerusalem. Lk 2:43

His parents did not know it, but supposing him to be in the company they went a day's journey, and sought him among their kinsfolk and acquaintances. And when they did not find him, they returned to Jerusalem, seeking him. Lk 2:43-45

After three days they found him in the temple, sitting among the teachers, listening to them and asking them questions. Lk 2:46

And all who heard him were amazed at his understanding and his answers. Lk 2:47

When they saw him they were astonished; and his mother said to him, "Son, why have you treated us so? Behold, your father and I have been looking for you anxiously." Lk 2:48

And he said to them, "How is it that you sought me? Did you not know that I must be in my father's house?" Lk 2:49

And they did not understand the saying which he spoke to them. Lk 2:50

He went with them and came to Nazareth, and was obedient to them. Lk 2:51

And his mother kept all these things, pondering them in her heart. Lk 2:51

Rosary journal

As you meditate on the mysteries of the Rosary, feel free to note any insights you have about the lives of Jesus and Mary – and/or how yours relates to theirs.

The Luminous Mysteries

The First Luminous Mystery
The Baptism of the Lord

John the baptizer appeared in the wilderness, preaching a baptism of repentance for the forgiveness of sins. Mk 1:4

"I baptize you with water for repentance, but he who is coming after me is mightier than I…he will baptize you with the Holy Spirit and with fire." Mt 3:11

"For this I came baptizing with water, that he might be revealed to Israel" Jn 1:31

He saw Jesus coming toward him and said, "Behold, the Lamb of God, who takes away the sins of the world!" Jn 1:29

John would have prevented him saying, "I need to be baptized by you, and do you come to me?" Mt 3:14

But Jesus answered him and said, "Let it be so now, for thus it is fitting for us to fulfill all righteousness." Then he consented. Mt 3:15

When Jesus was baptized, he went up immediately from the water. Mt 3:16

And behold, the heavens were opened. Mt 3:16

And the Holy Spirit descended upon him in bodily form, as a dove. Lk 3:22

And a voice came from heaven, "Thou art my beloved Son; with thee I am well pleased." Mk 1:11

The Second Luminous Mystery
The Wedding of Cana

On the third day there was a marriage at Cana in Galilee, and the mother of Jesus was there. Jesus was also invited to the marriage, with his disciples. Jn 2:1-2

When the wine failed, the mother of Jesus said to him, "They have no wine." Jn 2:3

And Jesus said to her, "O woman, what have you to do with me? My hour has not yet come." Jn 2:4

His mother said to the servants, "Do whatever he tells you." Jn 2:5

Now six stone jars were standing there, for the Jewish rites of purification, each holding twenty or thirty gallons. Jesus said to them, "Fill the jars with water." And they filled them up to the brim. Jn 2:6-7

He said, "Now draw some out, and take it to the steward of the feast." So they took it. Jn 2:8

The steward of the feast tasted the water now become wine, and did not know where it had come from (though the servants who had drawn the water knew). Jn 2:9

The steward of the feast called the bridegroom and said to him, "Every man serves the good wine first; and when men have drunk freely, then the poor wine; but you have kept the good wine until now." Jn 2:9-10

This, the first of his signs, Jesus did at Cana in Galilee, and manifested his glory. Jn 2:11

And his disciples believed in him. Jn 2:11

Rosary journal

As you meditate on the mysteries of the Rosary, feel free to note any insights you have about the lives of Jesus and Mary – and/or how yours relates to theirs.

Prayer Requests

As you pray the Rosary, you can lift up the things that you and your loved ones need. You can pray for the world. Consider listing your prayer requests.

The Third Luminous Mystery

The Proclamation of the Kingdom of God

Jesus came into Galilee, preaching the gospel of God, and saying, "The time is fulfilled, and the kingdom of God is at hand."
Mk 1:14-15

"Repent, and believe in the gospel." Mk 1:15

"The seed is the word of God…And as for that in the good soil, they are those who, hearing the word, hold it fast in an honest and good heart, and bring forth fruit with patience." Lk 8:11, 15

"The kingdom of heaven is like a grain of mustard seed which a man took and sowed in his field; it is the smallest of seeds." Mt 13:31

"But when it is grown it becomes the greatest of shrubs and is like a tree, so that the birds of the air come and make nests in its branches." Mt 13:32

"The kingdom of heaven is like a merchant in search of fine pearls who, on finding one pearl of great value, went and sold all that he had and bought it." Mt 13:45-46

"Unless you turn and become like children, you will never enter the kingdom of heaven." Mt 18:3

"Her sins which are many, are forgiven, for she has loved much"…Then he said to her, "Your sins are forgiven." Lk 7:47, 48

"If you forgive men their trespasses, your heavenly Father will also forgive you. Mt 6:14

He breathed on them and said to them, "Receive the Holy Spirit. If you forgive the sins of any, they are forgiven; if you retain the sins of any, they are retained." Jn 20:23

The Fourth Luminous Mystery

The Transfiguration

Jesus took with him Peter and James and John, and took them up a high mountain apart by themselves. Mk 9:2

And as he was praying, the appearance of his countenance was altered. Lk 9:29

And he was transfigured before them, and his face shone like the sun, and his garments became white as light. Mt 17:2

May God be gracious to us and bless us, and make his face to shine upon us. Ps 67:1

My heart says to thee, "Thy face, Lord, do I seek." Ps 27:8

Two men talked with him, Moses and Elijah, who appeared in glory and spoke of his departure, which he was to accomplish in Jerusalem. Lk 9:30-31

And as the men were parting from him, Peter said to Jesus, "Master, it is well we are here, let us make three booths, one for you, one for Moses, and one for Elijah" – not knowing what he said. Lk 9:33

He was still speaking, when lo, a bright cloud overshadowed them. Mt 17:5

And a voice came out of the cloud, "This is my beloved Son; listen to him." Mk 9:7

And suddenly looking around they no longer saw anyone with them but Jesus only. Mk 9:8

Rosary journal

As you meditate on the mysteries of the Rosary, feel free to note any insights you have about the lives of Jesus and Mary – and/or how yours relates to theirs.

Prayer Requests

As you pray the Rosary, you can lift up the things that you and your loved ones need. You can pray for the world. Consider listing your prayer requests.

The Fifth Luminous Mystery
The Institution of the Eucharist

Jesus sent Peter and John, saying, "Go and prepare the Passover for us, that we may eat it." Lk 22:8

And when the hour came, he sat at table, and the apostles with him. And he said to them, "I have earnestly desired to eat this Passover with you before I suffer." Lk 22:14-15

And he took bread, and when he had given thanks, he broke it and gave it to them, saying, "This is my body which is given for you." Lk 22:19

"The bread of God is that which comes down from heaven, and gives life to the world." Jn 6:33

"If anyone eats this bread, he will live forever; and the bread which I shall give for the life of the world is my flesh." Jn 6:51

And he took a cup, and when he had given thanks, he gave it to them, saying, "Drink of it, all of you; for this is the blood of the covenant which is poured out for many for the forgiveness of sins." Mt 26:27

"He who eats my flesh and drinks my blood has eternal life, and I will raise him up at the last day." Jn 6:54

"For my flesh is true food, and my blood is true drink." Jn 6:55

"Do this is remembrance of me." Lk 22:19

For as often as you eat this bread and drink the cup, you proclaim the Lord's death until he comes. 1 Cor 11:26

The First Sorrowful Mystery
The Agony in the Garden

They went to a place called Gethsemane…And he took with him Peter and James and John, and began to be greatly distressed and troubled.
Mk 14:32, 33

And he withdrew from them about a stone's throw, and knelt down and prayed, "Father, if thou art willing, remove this cup from me."
Lk 22:42

"Nevertheless, not my will, but thine, be done." Lk 22:42

And there appeared to him an angel from heaven, strengthening him.
Lk 22:43

And being in agony, he prayed more earnestly. Lk 22:44

And his sweat became like great drops of blood falling upon the ground. Lk 22:44

And he came to the disciples and found them sleeping; and he said to Peter, "So you could not watch with me one hour?" Mt 26:40

"Watch and pray that you may not enter into temptation; the spirit indeed is willing, but the flesh is weak." Mt 26:41

While he was still speaking, Judas came…and with him a crowd with swords and clubs…And he kissed him. And they laid hands on him and seized him. Mk 14:45, 46

Then all the disciples forsook him and fled. Mt 26:56

The Sorrowful Mysteries

Prayer Requests

As you pray the Rosary, you can lift up the things that you and your loved ones need. You can pray for the world. Consider listing your prayer requests.

Collection of Grace

The Second Sorrowful Mystery
The Scourging at the Pillar

Then Pilate took Jesus and scourged him. Jn 19:1

I gave my back to the smiters. Is 50:6

The plowers plowed upon my back; they made long their furrows. Ps 129:3

We esteemed him stricken, smitten by God, and afflicted. Is 53:4

He was wounded for our transgressions, bruised for our iniquities. Is 53:5

Yet it was the will of God to bruise him. Is 53:10

His appearance was so marred, beyond human semblance. Is 52:14

Upon him was the chastisement that made us whole. Is 53:5

And with his stripes we are healed. Is 53:5

Having scourged Jesus, Pilate delivered him over to be crucified. Mk 15:15

The Third Sorrowful Mystery
The Crowning with Thorns

The soldiers of the governor took Jesus into the praetorium, and they gathered the whole battalion before him. Mt 27:27

They stripped him and put a scarlet robe upon him. Mt 27:28

And plating a crown of thorns they put it on his head. Mt 27:29

And kneeling before him they mocked him saying, "Hail, King of the Jews!" Mt 27:29

And they struck his head with a reed and spat upon him. Mk 15:19

I hid not my face from shame and spitting. Is 50:6

Like a lamb that is led to the slaughter…so he opened not his mouth. Is 53:7

Jesus came out, wearing the crown of thorns and the purple robe. Pilate said to them, "Here is the man!" Jn 19:5

When the chief priests and the officers saw him, they cried out, "Crucify him! Crucify him!" Jn 19:6

And when they had mocked him, they stripped him of the robe, and put his own clothes on him, and led him away to crucify him. Mt 27:31

Rosary journal

As you meditate on the mysteries of the Rosary, feel free to note any insights you have about the lives of Jesus and Mary – and/or how yours relates to theirs.

Prayer Requests

As you pray the Rosary, you can lift up the things that you and your loved ones need. You can pray for the world. Consider listing your prayer requests.

The Fourth Sorrowful Mystery

Jesus Carries his Cross

They took Jesus, and he went out, bearing his own cross. Jn 19:17

Surely, he has borne our griefs and carried our sorrows. Is 53:4

He bore the sin of many and made intercession for the transgressors. Is 53:12

They seized one Simon of Cyrene, who was coming in from the country, and laid on him the cross to carry it behind Jesus. Lk 23:26

"If any man would come after me, let him deny himself and take up his cross daily and follow me." Lk 9:23

"Take my yoke upon you, and learn from me." Mt 11:29

"For I am gentle and lowly in heart, and you will find rest for your souls." Mt 11:29

There followed him a great multitude of the people and of women who bewailed and lamented him. Lk 23:27

But Jesus said turning to them, "Daughters of Jerusalem, do not weep for me, but weep for yourselves and for your children." Lk 23:28

And they brought him to the place called Golgotha (which means the place of a skull). Mk 15:22

The Fifth Sorrowful Mystery

The Death of Our Lord

When they came to the place called The Skull, there they crucified him. Lk 23:33

And Jesus said, "Father, forgive them, for they know not what they do." Lk 23:34

The rulers scoffed at him saying, "He saved others; let him save himself if he is the Christ of God, his Chosen One!" Lk 23:35

Standing by the cross of Jesus were his mother, and his mother's sister, Mary the wife of Clopas, and Mary Magdelene. John 19:25

When Jesus saw his mother and the disciple whom he loved standing near, he said to his mother, "Woman, behold your son!" Jn 19:26

Then he said to his disciple, "Behold, your mother!" And from that hour the disciple took her into his own home. Jn 19:27

After this Jesus, knowing that all was now finished, said (to fulfill the scripture), "I thirst." Jn 19:28

Jesus cried out with a loud voice, "Eli, Eli, lama sabachthani?" that is, "My God, my God, why hast thou forsaken me?" Mt 27:46

Then Jesus, crying out with a loud voice, said, "Father, into thy hands I commit my spirit!" And having said this he breathed his last. Lk 23:46

One of the soldiers pierced his side with a spear, and at once there came out blood and water. Jn 19:34

Rosary journal

As you meditate on the mysteries of the Rosary, feel free to note any insights you have about the lives of Jesus and Mary – and/or how yours relates to theirs.

The Glorious Mysteries

The First Glorious Mystery
The Resurrection

Now after the Sabbath, toward the dawn of the first day of the week, Mary Magdelene and the other Mary went to see the sepulchre. Mt 28:1

And they found the stone rolled back from the tomb, but when they went in, they did not find the body. Lk 24:3

Behold, two men stood by them in dazzling apparel and…said to them, "Why do you seek the living among the dead? He is not here, but has risen." Lk 24:5

They departed from the tomb with fear and great joy, and ran to tell his disciples. And behold, Jesus met them and said, "Hail!" Mt 28:8-9

And they came up and took hold of his feet and worshiped him. Mt 28:9

After this he appeared in another form to two of them as they were walking in the country. Mk 16:12

When he was at table with them, he took the bread and blessed, and broke it, and gave it to them. And their eyes were opened and they recognized him. Lk 24:30-31

On the evening of that day, the first day of the week, the doors being shut where the disciples were, for fear of the Jews, Jesus came and stood among them and said to them, "Peace be with you." Jn 20:19

He said to Thomas, "Put your finger here and see my hands; and put out your hand, and place it in my side; do not be faithless, but believing." Jn 20:27

Thomas answered him, "My Lord and my God!" Jn 20:28

The Second Glorious Mystery

The Ascension of Our Lord

Now the eleven disciples went to Galilee, to the mountain to which Jesus had directed them. Mt 28:16

Jesus came and said to them, "…Go…and make disciples of all nations, baptizing them in the name of the Father and of the Son and of the Holy Spirit." Mt 28:18,19

"It is to your advantage that I go away, for if I do not go away, the Holy Spirit will not come to you; but if I go, I will send him to you." Jn 16:7

"Behold, I send the promise of my Father upon you; but stay in the city, until you are clothed with power from on high." Luke 24:49

And lifting up his hands he blessed them. While he blessed them, he parted from them and was taken up into heaven. Lk 24:50, 51

As they were looking on he was lifted up, and a cloud took him out of their sight. Acts 1:9

The Lord Jesus…was taken up into heaven, and sat down at the right hand of God. Mk 16:19

Seek the things that are above, where Christ is, seated at the right hand of God. Col 3:1

"In my Father's house are many rooms; if it were not so, would I have told you that I go to prepare a place for you?" Jn 14:2

And while they were gazing up into heaven as he went, behold, two men stood by them in white robes, and said, "…This Jesus, who was taken up into heaven, will come in the same way as you saw him go into heaven." Acts 1:10, 11

Rosary journal

As you meditate on the mysteries of the Rosary, feel free to note any insights you have about the lives of Jesus and Mary – and/or how yours relates to theirs.

Prayer Requests

As you pray the Rosary, you can lift up the things that you and your loved ones need. You can pray for the world. Consider listing your prayer requests.

The Third Glorious Mystery
The Descent of the Holy Spirit

They returned to Jerusalem from the mount called Olivet…All these with one accord devoted themselves to prayer together with the women and Mary the mother of Jesus, and with his brethren. Acts 1:12, 14

When the day of Pentecost had come, they were all together in one place. Acts 2:1

And suddenly a sound came from heaven like the rush of mighty wind, and it filled all the house where they were sitting. Acts 2:2

And there appeared tongues as of fire, distributed and resting on each one of them. Acts 2:3

And they were all filled with the Holy Spirit. Acts 2:4

And [they] began to speak in tongues as the Spirit gave them utterance. Acts 2:4

Now there were in Jerusalem Jews, devout men from every nation under heaven. And at this sound they came together, and they were bewildered, because each one heard them speaking in his own language. Acts 2:5-6

And Peter said to them, "Repent, and be baptized every one of you in the name of Jesus Christ for the forgiveness of sins; and you shall receive the gift of the Holy Spirit." Acts 2:38

So those who received his word were baptized, and there were added that day about three thousand souls. Acts 2:41

And they devoted themselves to the apostles' teaching and fellowship, to the breaking of bread and the prayers. Acts 2:42

The Fourth Glorious Mystery

The Assumption of the Blessed Virgin Mary

She is a reflection of eternal light, a spotless mirror of the working of God, and an image of his goodness. Ws 7:26

"When I go and prepare a place for you, I will come again and will take you to myself, that where I am you may be also." Jn 14:3

Arise, O Lord, and go to thy resting place, thou and the ark of thy might. Ps 132:8

My beloved speaks and says to me, "Arise, my love, my fair one, and come away; for lo, the winter is past, and the rain is over and gone." Song 2:10

The woman was given two wings of the great eagle that she might fly from the serpent into the wilderness, to a place where she is to be nourished. Rev 12:14

Draw me after you. Let us make haste. The king has brought me into his chambers. Song 1:4

Rejoice and exult with all your heart, O daughter of Jerusalem…The King of Israel, the Lord, is in your midst. Zeph 3:14, 15

"O daughter, you are blessed by the Most High above all women on earth." Jud 13:18

"Behold, henceforth all generations will call me blessed." Lk 1:48

"For he who is mighty has done great things for me, and holy is his name." Lk 1:49

Rosary journal

As you meditate on the mysteries of the Rosary, feel free to note any insights you have about the lives of Jesus and Mary – and/or how yours relates to theirs.

Prayer Requests

As you pray the Rosary, you can lift up the things that you and your loved ones need. You can pray for the world. Consider listing your prayer requests.

The Fifth Glorious Mystery
The Crowning of Mary Queen of Heaven and Earth

The Lord takes pleasure in his people; he adorns the humble with victory. Ps 149:4

He has clothed me with the garments of salvation, he has covered me with the robe of righteousness. Is 61:10

Henceforth there is laid up for me the crown of righteousness, which the Lord, the righteous judge, will award me. 2 Tim 4:8

Rejoice greatly, O daughter of Zion! Shout aloud, O daughter of Jerusalem! Lo, your king comes to you. Zech 9:9

A great portent appeared in the heaven, a woman clothed with the sun, with the moon under her feet. Rev 12:1

And on her head a crown of twelve stars Rev 12:1

The king rose to meet her, and bowed down to her; then he sat on his throne, and had a seat brought for the king's mother; and she sat on his right. 1 Kg 2:19

You are the exaltation of Jerusalem, you are the great glory of Israel, you are the greatest pride of our nation! Jud 15:9

Who is this that looks forth like the dawn, fair as the moon, bright as the sun, terrible as an army with banners? Song 6:10

I am the mother of beautiful love, of fear, of knowledge, and of holy hope. Sir 24:18

My *Flexible* Plan

Come pray with your family around the world! Which prayers of the Church will help you at this season of your life? You can include page numbers or prayer titles or your own reflections.

How shall I incorporate the prayers of the Church into my own prayers?

❑ Common Catholic prayers:

❑ Mass:

❑ Longer prayers or litanies:

❑ Rosary:

❑ Other ideas:

Dear God, you know that my background with church is...

And at this point in my life, I would like to grow in praying with the Church by...

I will need your help because...

Love,

Chapter 6

With and For Others

When I first went to college, the internet was just about to pick up popularity. Students were given an email address – new concept to us all. My parents jumped on board and got an email address so that we could communicate more easily over the 1000 miles between us. Writing to them was one of my favorite things about college. Not only was I able to contemplate at the keyboard all the things that were going on around and within me via this new life, but I was able to share it with people who loved me. They reacted, then encouraged, they questioned.

Prayers can be like this too. They can be full of your own wonder and connection to God in a way that others can also enter into that conversation. In prayer, we come to know ourselves better. Yet our self-knowledge matters little compared with the wonderful relationship which is formed with God in the midst of that growth. And our relationship with God is formed in community. We image God more fully when we are together. Through community, with God as our king, we begin to get a taste of heaven.

The gardens of our front yards are not only made up of one plant and neither is the garden of the Lord. We complement each other; we lift each other up; we are more interesting as a full body. Let's enjoy that full garden of grace with others, in community through petition, praise and healing. Here are some resources to help you more easily connect in prayer.

Who are the people in your faith community?

This may be a diverse mix of people who do not know each other. The community of faith is huge and transcends time.

Who . . .

Builds you up _____
How? When?

Has inspiring faith_____
How? When?

Reminds you to care for people
who are in need _____
How? When?

By your side during difficult times
How? When? _____

Worships God with you
How? When? _____

Prays out load _____
How? When?

Your experience

What is your experience with prayer along with other people? Have you done any of these common prayers? When, how, where? What goes on in your heart and mind during this kind of prayer?

What about this type of prayer? When, how, where? What goes on in your heart and mind during this kind of prayer?

Prayer with Others

There is something very special about prayer with others. Jesus said, "Where two or three are gathered in my name, there am I in the midst of them." Almost any prayer in this book can be done with others but those in this chapter are easily suited for groups.

Common Prayers for Praying Together
Our Father
Meal Time Grace
The Rosary
The Chaplet of Divine Mercy
The Angelus
The Regina Coeli
Prayers of the Faithful
The Prayer to the Holy Spirit
Songs and Hymns
Liturgy of the Hours

From the Heart – Extemporaneously as a Group
It takes either leadership or culture to pray well as a group. And of course, a work of God. Here are a few tips to create that environment when praying extemporaneously.

The ABC's of Prayer
A - be Audible
B - be Brief (less than a minute per person)
C - be Christ centered

Mode Options:
popcorn style - whenever someone has an idea, they pray it.
in a circle - make sure to let people pass if they don't have anything to say.
after three - have three people volunteer to pray for the group's needs, then you all say "amen."
opener and closer - designate one person to start everyone off and one person to discern when the group is done and then to say a closing prayer.

Family Prayer

This is a format you can use to pray with your family or friends. It takes about 10-20 minutes and can be adapted to all sorts of ages and conditions.

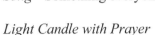

Song - Something everyone can sing…

Light Candle with Prayer
Leader: "This candle reminds us that Jesus is with us."
All: "Jesus, you are welcome here."
Leader: "We come together as a family to love you, to listen to you and to be filled up with you."

Message
Deliver a good short message to the family using the bible, a book, art, conversation.

Pondering
Try to discover what the message's challenge or encouragement is for these particular individuals. Together consider: What do you think this means? How can you apply this in your life?

Prayerful Response
Leader suggests one simple sentence for each person to pray regarding the message. For example, each person in the circle can say,
"Thank you, God, you have …" or "I praise you God because…"
"Please help me to …"

Intercessions
Pray for the needs of the world – near and far. Each person can say a petition and all can respond, "Lord hear our prayer" or something similar.

Blessing
Dad prays: "May the Lord bless you and keep you.
May he make his face shine upon you and be gracious to you.
May he look upon you and give you peace."
Each person blesses everyone with a cross on the forehead and says: "Bless you."

Awkward Moments made better

With a pattern, routine or ritual, people know when to stand for the "wave" at a ball game, what to do when you introduce your family to a friend, what to do at a dinner table.

At first, learning a ritual can be awkward but once it becomes habit, it is second nature.

What formats, patterns or rituals do you have with your family or close fiend group which helps you to function easier? What small habit, signal or ritual could your family start so that you could pray together (even a tiny bit) with some ease?

Memorize it

Pick the call and response which most resonates with you. Write it over and over in the space below. Then, cover it up and see if you have it memorized. Try to say it tomorrow at about this time.

Call and Response

Memorized Scripture serves as an easy communal prayer. Use these call and responses with just two people or a whole group. After the verse, you can each pray extemporaneously for a bit or if you are short on time, skip that part.

Praise   (1 Chronicles 16:34)
Call: *Give thanks to the Lord for he is good.*
Response: *His love endures forever.*

Thank you, Jesus for…
Praise you, Lord, you are…

Confess   (Psalm 51:10)
Call: *Create in me a pure heart, O God,*
Response: *and renew a steadfast spirit within me.*

Lord, I'm sorry for…
Please forgive me and heal me…

Ask   (Matthew 7:7)
Call: *Ask and it will be given to you;*
Response: *seek and you will find.*

Please help (me & others) …

Receive   (1 Samuel 3:10)
Call: *The Lord came and stood there,*
     calling as at the other times…
Response: *speak, for your servant is listening.*

Read a paragraph from a spiritual book or be silent

Consecrate   (Luke 1:38)
Call: *Behold, I am the servant of the Lord:*
Response: *be it done unto me according to your word.*

God, I dedicate to you …

From the Heart – Praying with a Prayer Partner

During a few special seasons in my life, I've been blessed with a "prayer partner." Below is an explanation of how it usually would unfold. You could pray this way anytime with a close Christian friend. It doesn't have to be something official.

1. Briefly ask God to bless your time together.

2. One person shares for 5-10 minutes about the ups and downs of her current circumstances and the direction her mind and heart are going.

3. The other person listens and responds naturally.

4. The other person shares and the first friend listens and shares naturally.

5. Pray about it together for 5-10 minutes. Each person takes turns relaying to God something specific about what has been said in discussion. Example:

   "Father, my friend is grieving in her heart about the fighting and chaos in her home. She feels like anything she does to bring people together just ends up falling apart. Please help her when she is conversing with her kids. Give her insight into their feelings and extend your compassion to her family through her."

6. The other person adds on to that particular prayer and brings up another. Example:

   "Yes, Lord, please increase the love in my heart for my family and help me to see more clearly. Thank you for the new job you have given my friend. Bring your peace to her work place, especially as she interacts with the receptionist. May your Spirit be in between them."

7. Praise and thank God for his presence with you.

Good Qualities

Describe the qualities of a person who would make a good prayer partner for you.

How do YOU match up

to those qualities? What would someone need from you?

Pray that God will open doors for someone to be a praying friend to you. Pray that you might become someone who could do that for another.

Who needs help?

We gather as a church to intercede on behalf of others. List the needs of the world (personal, local, national, global). Write as many things as will fit in this space.

Petition and Healing

Christians are called to reach out to the world. Our prayers make a difference. Likewise, Jesus said, we would do greater things than him! Through the Holy Spirit, we too can heal the sick, comfort the afflicted and bring life where there is none.

Prayers of the Faithful

After the readings at Mass, we pray for the needs of the world. In your own home, or small group, you can do something similar.

According to the General Instruction of the Roman Missal, the series of intentions is usually to be:

1. for the needs of the Church
2. for public authorities and the salvation of the whole world
3. for those burdened by any kind of difficulty
4. for the local community

For example: The Response is, *Lord hear our prayer*

For the whole Church:
that we may be united by the Holy Spirit in truth and love so as to bring life to this world, we pray to the Lord:

For leaders around world:
that they might find ways to end to war and violence, and promote peace and development for all nations, we pray to the Lord:

For those tempted to despair by constant pain:
that they might join their suffering to the Cross of Christ and find consolation, we pray to the Lord:

For those in our community who struggle to make ends meet,
that they may have the support they need,
we pray to the Lord.

142

Intentions of Our Holy Father

Each month, the Pope presents something for which he is praying for in particular. We can join our prayers to his. Here is an example:

January - We pray that Christians, followers of other religions, and all people of goodwill may promote peace and justice in the world.

February - We pray that the cries of our migrant brothers and sisters, victims of criminal trafficking, may be heard and considered.

March - We pray that the Church in China may persevere in its faithfulness to the Gospel and grow in unity.

April - We pray that those suffering from addiction may be helped and accompanied.

May - We pray that deacons, faithful in their service to the Word and the poor, may be an invigorating symbol for the entire Church.

June - We pray that all those who suffer may find their way in life, allowing themselves to be touched by the Heart of Jesus.

July - We pray that today's families may be accompanied with love, respect and guidance.

August - We pray for all those who work and live from the sea, among them sailors, fishermen and their families.

September - We pray that the planet's resources will not be plundered, but shared in a just and respectful manner.

October - We pray that by the virtue of baptism, the laity, especially women, may participate more in areas of responsibility in the Church.

November - We pray that the progress of robotics and artificial intelligence may always serve humankind.

December - We pray that our personal relationship with Jesus Christ be nourished by the Word of God and a life of prayer.

The prayer of a good person has a powerful effect.

- James 5:16 (GNT)

Who is God?

In the first two paragraphs, read the description of the characteristics of God to whom Pope Francis is petitioning. Underline the parts which refer to who God is.

Describe the characteristics of God whom *you know and petition.* If you are compelled by what you read, feel free to incorporate some of Pope Francis' language but...

be true to what you know
of God in your heart.

Pope Francis' Litany of Supplications
This world prayed this together during the Urbi et Orbi blessing on March 27, 2020. It is a good prayer for every day we struggle here.

Response: *We adore you, O Lord*
True God and true Man, truly present in this holy Sacrament R
Our Savior, God with us, faithful and rich in mercy R
King and Lord of Creation and of history R
Conqueror of sin and death R
Friend of humankind, the Risen One,
the living one who sits at the right hand of the Father R

Response: *We believe in you, O Lord*
Only begotten Son of the Father
descended from heaven for our salvation R
Heavenly physician, who bows down over our misery R
Lamb who was slain who offered yourself to rescue us from evil R
Good Shepherd, who give your life for the flock which you love R
Living Bread and medicine for immortality who give us Eternal Life

Response: *Deliver us, O Lord*
From the power of Satan and the seductions of the world R
From the pride and presumption of being able
to do anything without You R
From the deceptions of fear and anxiety R
From unbelief and desperation R
From hardness of heart and the incapacity to love R

Response: *Save us, O Lord*
From every evil that afflicts humanity R
From hunger, from famine, and from egoism R
From illnesses, epidemics, and the fear of our brothers and sisters R
From devastating madness, from ruthless interests
and from violence R
From being deceived, from false information
and the manipulation of consciences R

Response: *Comfort us, O Lord*
Protect your Church which crosses the desert R
Protect humanity, terrified by fear and anguish R
Protect the sick and the dying, oppressed by loneliness R

Protect doctors and healthcare workers,
exhausted by the difficulties they are facing R
Protect politicians and decision makers
who bear the weight of having to make decisions R

Response: *Grant us your Spirit, O Lord*
In the Hour of trial and from confusion R
In temptation and in our fragility R
In the battle against evil and sin R
In the search for what is truly good and true joy R
In the decision to remain in you and in your friendship R

Response: *Open us to hope, O Lord*
Should sin oppress us R
Should hatred close our hearts R
Should sorrow visit us R
Should indifference cause us anguish R
Should death overwhelm us R

From the Heart – Asking for Help
Of course, God wants to hear straight from us when we are grieving or when we intercede for another person.

Tell God honestly what is going on, the way you would tell a loved one. Don't be afraid to show your emotions to the Lord. Ask simply for what you and others need. Your prayer can be short and to the point or can be a long expression.

Arrow Prayers
When you walk around during the day, you see all sorts of things that grieve your heart or call to you for intercession. One of my friends taught me to consider a few of these simple phrases as part of an arsenal to spontaneously fire off on behalf of others.

God, please help that person.
Your love for these people is great.
Please bring conversion/healing/trust/ a miracle.
Praise you, God for you will do great things for them.

Spill it...
Everyone needs to share frequently but many of us don't have the relationship dynamics that make it easy.

Where do you feel most comfortable talking about your life, your feelings, your angst and hopes? Check as many boxes as apply. There is no "right" answer.

❑ anytime, anywhere

❑ when I'm exercising

❑ late at night

❑ when no one else is listening

❑ when I write

❑ when someone else asks the right questions

❑ over a meal

❑ when someone else is vulnerable with me

❑ whenever something is "off"

take this **self-knowledge** and **translate** it to your conversation with God

People you love

Who in your life has been seriously ill or injured? Write about it:

Prayers for a Sick Person

It is very common for us to pray _for_ people who are sick but uncommon to pray _with_ people who are sick. Try praying this prayer with an ailing person.

Gentle Jesus, you healed the sick, cured the blind and raised the dead. Please send your Spirit upon _____.
Heal him/her in mind, body and soul.
If it be the Father's will, please take away his/her infirmity.
Give him/her the comfort of your presence.
Just as life came from your death and resurrection,
may tremendous goodness come from the experience
that _____ is going through. Help us, Lord.

Petition Ideas

Praying for others does not come easily for you? Here are some ideas.

- Kneel by your bedside and ask about your concerns.
- Divine Mercy Chaplet – for each bead, say the name of someone suffering
- Rosary – in the beginning of each mystery, make your requests known to God
- Around the dinner table – mention someone you know who needs your prayers
- Go for a walk – pray for everything and everyone you pass by
- Cry out to God for an extended time on behalf of someone who is struggling. Tell God everything possible.
- Offer up each struggle during the day for people whom you love.
- Write a letter to God on behalf of a friend and e-mail it to her.
- Visualize all of your loved ones at the foot of the altar. Ask God's blessing on them.
- Trace a small cross on the forehead of the person for whom you are praying.
- Read the newspaper and pray during each article.

Hymns

Music can tremendously amplify your prayer life and the life of a community. Many times, the best mealtime grace, family prayer or personal devotion is a song.   Here are a few hymns in the public domain to get you started.

Amazing Grace

Amazing Grace,
how sweet the sound,
That saved a wretch like me.
I once was lost
but now am found,
Was blind, but now I see.

T'was Grace that taught
my heart to fear.
And Grace, my fears relieved.
How precious did
that Grace appear
The hour I first believed.

Through many dangers,
toils and snares
I have already come;
'Tis Grace that brought
me safe thus far
and Grace will lead me home.

When we've been here
ten thousand years
Bright shining as the sun.
We've no less days
to sing God's praise
Than when we've first begun.

Father, I Adore You

Father, I adore You
Lay my life before You
How I love You
Jesus, I adore You…
Spirit, I adore You…

Rock Of Ages

Rock of Ages, cleft for me,
Let me hide myself in Thee;
Let the water and the blood,
From Thy wounded side
which flowed,
Be of sin the double cure;
Save from wrath and make me
pure.

Not the labor of my hands
Can fulfill Thy law's demands;
Could my zeal no respite know,
Could my tears forever flow,
All for sin could not atone;
Thou must save, and Thou alone.

Nothing in my hand I bring,
Simply to the cross I cling;
Naked, come to Thee for dress;
Helpless look to Thee for grace;
Foul, I to the fountain fly;
Wash me, Savior, or I die.

While I draw this fleeting breath,
When mine eyes
shall close in death,
When I soar to worlds unknown,
See Thee on Thy judgment throne,
Rock of Ages, cleft
for me,
Let me hide
myself in
Thee

He who sings prays twice

-Attributed to St. Augustine

What are some benefits of singing?
List 10 benefits to:

Singing (in general)

1.

2.

3.

4.

5.

Singing with others

6.

7.

8.

9.

10.

Listen

to a few of these songs and sing along. You can find them on YouTube, google, Spotify etc. The songs here are all old and in the public domain but there are also many modern songs which lift our hearts to God.

Do a little research and list 3 modern worship songs.

Title and Artist

1.

2.

3.

Collection of Grace

Panis Angelicus
By St. Thomas Aquinas

Panis angelicus
fit panis hominum;
Dat panis cœlicus
figuris terminum:
O res mirabilis!
Manducat Dominum
Pauper, Pauper,
servus et humilis.

Te trina Deitas
unaque poscimus:
Sic nos tu visita,
sicut te colimus;
Per tuas semitas
duc nos quo tendimus,
Ad lucem quam inhabitas.

May the Bread of Angels
Become bread for mankind;
The Bread of Heaven puts
All foreshadowings to an end;
Oh, thing miraculous!
The body of the Lord will nourish
the poor, the poor,
the servile, and the humble.

You God, Three In One,
we beseech;
That You visit us,
As we worship You.
By Your ways,
lead us where we are heading,
to the light that You inhabitest.

Come Holy Ghost
Come Holy Ghost,
Creator blest
And in our hearts
take up Thy rest
Come with Thy grace
and heavenly aid
To fill the hearts
which Thou hast made (2x)

O Comfort blest,
to Thee we cry
Thou heavenly Gift
of God most High
Thou Font of life
and Fire of love
And sweet Anointing
from above (2x)

Praise be to Thee,
Father and Son
And Holy Spirit
Three in One
And may the Son
on us bestow
The gifts that from
the Spirit flow (2x)

Lift High the Cross
Lift high the cross,
the love of Christ proclaim,
Till all the world
adore His sacred Name.

Led on their way
by this triumphant sign,
The hosts of God
in conquering ranks combine.

Be Thou My Vision

Be Thou my Vision,
O Lord of my heart;
Naught be all else to me,
save that Thou art
Thou my best Thought,
by day or by night,
Waking or sleeping,
Thy presence my light.

Be Thou my Wisdom,
and Thou my true Word;
I ever with Thee
and Thou with me, Lord;
Thou my great Father,
I Thy true son;
Thou in me dwelling,
and I with Thee one. (2x)

Riches I heed not,
nor man's empty praise,
Thou mine Inheritance,
now and always:
Thou and Thou only,
first in my heart,
High King of Heaven,
my Treasure Thou art. (2x)

High King of Heaven,
my victory won,
May I reach Heaven's joys,
O bright Heaven's Sun!
Heart of my own heart,
whatever befall,
Still be my Vision,
O Ruler of all.

O Sacrament Most Holy

O Sacrament most Holy,
O Sacrament Divine,
All praise and all thanksgiving,
Be every moment Thine.

Holy Holy Holy

Holy, holy, holy!
Lord God Almighty!
Early in the morning
our song shall rise to Thee;
Holy, holy, holy,
merciful and mighty!
God in three Persons,
blessed Trinity!

Holy, holy, holy!
All the saints adore Thee,
Casting down their golden
crowns around the glassy sea;
Cherubim and seraphim
falling down before Thee,
Who was, and is,
and evermore shall be.

Holy, holy, holy!
though the darkness hide Thee,
Though the eye of sinful man
Thy glory may not see;
Only Thou art holy;
there is none beside Thee,
Perfect in power, in
love, and purity.

Holy, holy, holy!
Lord God Almighty!
All Thy works shall praise
Thy Name, in earth,
and sky, and sea;
Holy, holy, holy;
merciful and mighty!
God in three Persons,
blessed Trinity!

Do you sing or just pretend?

Some people are hesitant to sing. Do you feel any of these?

- ❑ I'm not a good singer
- ❑ Songs are usually too high
- ❑ My voice might crack
- ❑ I hope nobody hears me
- ❑ It exposes me too much
- ❑ Singing is embarrassing
- ❑ Singing in a crowd is fine
- ❑ Singing on my own by myself is fine

Open the door

When people take the risk of singing, they open the door to God, light, and joy. Likewise, you can "let yourself out" and find freedom and confidence.

What could help someone who is shy about singing?

What does that mean?

Look through the songs in this section. Find a few phrases (or a chorus) which seems interesting. Explain what it could mean in your life.

Lyrics

Meaning in your life

Holy God, We Praise Thy Name

Holy God,
we praise Thy Name;
Lord of all,
we bow before thee!
All on earth Thy scepter claim,
All in Heaven
above adore Thee;
Infinite Thy vast domain,
Everlasting is Thy reign.

Hark! the loud celestial hymn
Angel choirs above are raising,
Cherubim and seraphim ,
In unceasing chorus praising;
Fill the heavens
with sweet accord:
Holy, holy, holy, Lord.

Take My Life and Let It Be

Take my life, and let it be
consecrated, Lord, to Thee.
Take my moments
and my days;
let them flow
in ceaseless praise.
Take my hands
and let them move
at the impulse of Thy love.
Take my feet and let them be
swift and beautiful for Thee.

Take my will
and make it Thine;
it shall be no longer mine.
Take my heart, it is Thine own;
it shall be Thy royal throne.
Take my love,
my Lord, I pour at Thy feet
its treasure store.
Take myself, and I will be ever,
only, all for Thee.

It Is Well with My Soul

When peace, like a river,
attendeth my way,
When sorrows
like sea billows roll;
Whatever my lot,
Thou has taught me to say,
It is well, it is well,
with my soul.

It is well, with my soul,
It is well, with my soul,
It is well, it is well,
with my soul.

Though Satan should buffet,
though trials should come,
Let this blest assurance control,
That Christ has regarded
my helpless estate,
And hath shed His own blood
for my soul.

My sin, oh, the bliss of this
glorious thought!
My sin, not in part
but the whole,
Is nailed to the cross,
and I bear it no more,
Praise the Lord,
praise the Lord, O my soul!

And Lord, haste the day
when my faith shall be sight,
The clouds be rolled back
as a scroll;
The trump shall resound,
and the Lord shall descend,
Even so, it is well with my soul.

Precious Lord, Take My Hand

Precious Lord, take my hand
Lead me on, let me stand
I am tired, I am weak,
I am worn. Through the storm,
through the night,
Lead me on to the light

Take my hand, precious Lord,
lead me home

When my way grows drear,
Precious Lord, linger near,
When my life is almost gone
Hear my cry, hear my call
Hold my hand lest I fall

Take my hand, precious Lord,
lead me home

When the darkness appears
And the night draws near
And the day is past and gone
At the river I stand
Guide my feet, hold my hand
Take my hand, precious Lord,
lead me home (2x)

The Old Rugged Cross

On a hill far away stood
an old rugged cross,
The emblem of suffering
and shame;
And I love that old cross
where the dearest and best
For a world of lost sinners
was slain.

So I'll cherish
the old rugged cross,
Till my trophies at last
I lay down; I will cling
to the old rugged cross,
And exchange it some day
for a crown.

What A Friend We Have

What a friend we have in Jesus,
all our sins and griefs to bear!
What a privilege to carry
everything to God in prayer!
O what peace we often forfeit,
O what needless pain we bear,
all because we do not carry
everything to God in prayer.

Have we trials and temptations?
Is there trouble anywhere?
We should never be
discouraged;
take it to the Lord in prayer.
Can we find a friend so faithful
who will all our sorrows share?
Jesus knows
our every weakness;
take it to the Lord in prayer.

Are we weak and heavy laden,
cumbered with a load of care?
Precious Savior,
still our refuge;
take it to the Lord in prayer.
Do thy friends despise,
forsake thee?
Take it to the Lord in prayer!
In his arms he'll take
and shield thee;
thou wilt find a solace there.

What does that mean?

Find a phrase
that an elementary
school kid would
not understand.
Look up the words
and explain it here.

Lyrics

Explanation

Compose your own line of song or poem of praise.

Just lyrics are fine but if you want to (and know how) you could compose a melody and include chords here.

Collection of Grace

How Great Thou Art

O LORD my God!
When I in awesome wonder
Consider all
the works Thy hand
hath made;
I see the stars,
I hear the mighty thunder,

Then sings my soul,
my Saviour God, to Thee,
How great Thou art! (2x)
Then sings my soul,
my Saviour God, to Thee,
How great Thou art! (2x)

When through the woods
and forest glades I wander
And hear the birds
sing sweetly in the trees;
When I look down from
lofty mountain grandeur,
And hear the brook,
and feel the gentle breeze:

And when I think that God,
His Son not sparing,
Sent Him to die –
I scarce can take it in:
That on the Cross,
my burden gladly bearing,
He bled and died
to take away my sin:

When Christ shall come
with shout of acclamation
And take me home –
what joy shall fill my heart!
Then shall I bow
in humble adoration,
And there proclaim, my God
how great Thou art!

For All the Saints

For all the saints, who from
their labors rest,
Who Thee by faith before the
world confessed,
Thy Name, O Jesus,
be forever blessed.
Alleluia, Alleluia!

Thou wast their Rock, their
Fortress and their Might;
Thou, Lord, their Captain in the
well fought fight;
Thou, in the darkness drear,
their one true Light.
Alleluia, Alleluia!

Praise to the Lord, the Almighty, the King of Creation

O my soul, praise him, for he is
your health and salvation!
Come, all who hear: Brothers
and sisters, draw near,
Praise him in glad adoration!

Praise to the Lord,
above all things
so mightily reigning;
Keeping us safe at his side,
and so gently sustaining.
Have you not seen
all you have needed has been
Met by his gracious ordaining?

Praise to the Lord,
who shall prosper our work
and defend us;
Surely his goodness
and mercy shall daily attend us.
Ponder a new
what the Almighty can do,
Who with his love
will befriend us.

Immaculate Mary

Immaculate Mary,
thy praises we sing,
Who reignest in splendor
with Jesus our King.
Ave, Ave, Ave María!
Ave, Ave María!

In heaven the blessed
thy glory proclaim,
On earth we thy children
invoke thy fair name.
Ave, Ave, Ave María!
Ave, Ave María!

Thy name is our power,
thy virtues our light,
Thy love is our comfort,
thy pleading our might.
Ave, Ave, Ave, María!
Ave, Ave, María!

Hail Holy Queen Enthroned Above

Hail, Holy Queen
enthroned above, O Maria.
Hail, Queen of mercy
and of love, O Maria.

Triumph, all ye cherubim,
Sing with us, ye seraphim,
Heaven and earth
resound the hymn:
Salve, salve, salve Regina!

Our life, our sweetness,
here below, O Maria!
Our hope in sorrow
and in woe, O Maria!

Ave Maria
Bach / Gounod
Ave Maria
Gratia plena
Dominus tecum
Benedicta tu in mulieribus
Et benedictus fructus ventres
Tui Jesus
Sancta Maria, Sancta Maria
Maria
Ora pro nobis
Nobis peccatoribus
Nunc et in hora, in hora
Mortis nostrae

Ave Maria
Schubert
Ave Maria, gratia plena,
Maria, gratia plena,
Maria, gratia plena,
Ave, Ave, Dominus,
Dominus tecum.
Benedicta tu in mulieribus,
et benedictus,
Et benedictus
fructus ventris tui,
Ventris tui, Jesus.
Ave Maria!

Sancta Maria, Mater Dei,
Ora pro nobis peccatoribus,
Ora, ora
pro nobis;
Ora, ora
pro nobis peccatoribus,
Nunc et in hora mortis,
In hora mortis nostrae.
In hora, hora mortis nostrae,
In hora mortis nostrae.
Ave
Maria!
Amen,
Amen

Singing at church

When you sing at church, you give confidence and permission to the people around you to participate. Inhibition can be dropped so that all can be free and filled. When we sing, we give a gift to God of ourselves.

What does it take **externally** for you to sing freely? (what kind of an environment)

What does it take **internally**?

Answers to Prayers

God has answered many of the prayers we have said with and for others. Let us acknowledge that.

Your Presence is the Answer

Consider how God has been with you as you have praised him with others. How has he answered your prayers for the people you love?

A start for me would be, "Thank you, God, you saved our uncle from death. You made our family more peaceful. You changed red lights to green for me. You brought a friend to me 10,000 times when I needed one. You made it sunny. You let me and four of my kids stay alive because of modern medicine. You welcomed your arms my little unborn baby who passed away. You revived our community."

What about you? Here is space for you to write down some of the answers you have witnessed.

More journal space.

My *Flexible* Plan

God made your heart to be close to his and to his people. Write down some things that may help you pray with and for others. How can you experience a taste of heaven?

How can I pray more freely as an expression of my heart in community?

❏ Praying with others:

❏ Praying for healing:

❏ People to pray for:

❏ Song:

❏ Other ideas:

Dear God, I am a person who is connected to others by...

You know my personal preferences and see that I love to pray...

I want to openly express myself to you by...

I feel free with my brothers and sisters in Christ when...

Please help me...

Love,

Chapter 7

Finding Resources

In 1994, the Catechism of the Catholic Church came to my one room parish bookstore. Stooped on my knees looking at the lowest shelf, my hands trembled as I reached for the first time to touch the new, long awaited – Catechism.

The answers. So many questions. Here was a statement. Official. I paused in my low position, savoring the feel of the crushed carpet beneath my knees, the look of the windows and the smell of the 1950's building.

It is amazing what a resource can do for a person. It can be a friend at your most dire moment or that helpful insight that makes you chose a different path. For me, books have set me on fire and quenched my thirst. What about you? What resources delight you and help you to grow leaps and bounds?

Keep going in your life of prayer! There are so many resources available, most especially God himself and his Church. Being a continual student of the faith is a good way to keep growing. We all need sources of input- like a plant needs nourishment. In order to grow, we need new sources of inspiration; we need to keep stretching and learning. St. Josemaria said that for the modern apostle, one hour of study is equal to one hour of prayer. So, dig in!

"As you grow ready for it, somewhere or other, you will find what is needful for you in a book."

- George Macdonald

Classic Prayer Books

Here are some awesome prayer books to further your inner life and connect you with the body of Christ. Most of them are not "guided" in the way that <u>Collection of Grace</u> is, but they contain the best of the best content.

The Bible

The Catechism of the Catholic Church

Liturgy of the Hours (4-Volume Set)
by Catholic Book Publishing Co

Christian Prayer: The Liturgy of the Hours
by Catholic Book Publishing Co

Daily Office Readings Year 1, Volumes1&2
by Church Publishing,

Daily Roman Missal 3rd Edition
by Our Sunday Visitor

Your next step

While the resources on the right (p. 158) are excellent, some of them may need more guidance for you next step. Some people struggle with knowing what to do with them. There are some resources with have step by step guidance. Do a little research (perhaps on https://goodbooksforcatholickids.com/) and find one that will be good for your next step.

What do you choose?
Or, to what do you think God is leading you?

Vatican II Weekday Missal
by Daughters of St. Paul
The Vatican II Sunday Missal
by Daughters of St. Paul

Ordinary Work, Extraordinary Grace:
My Spiritual Journey in Opus Dei
by Scott Hahn

Handbook of Prayers
by James Socias

My Daily Bread
by Father Anthony J. Paone S.J.

Hearts on Fire: Praying with Jesuits
by Michael Harte

Authors for Study

Here are some of my favorite authors (both Catholic and Protestant) that will be challenging and helpful. I've tried to arrange them from least difficult to most. but it varies depending upon their works. They get into college level reading pretty quickly.

Matthew Kelly	C.S. Lewis
Katie Davis	J.R.R. Tolkien
Gary Chapman	G.K. Chesterton
Mother Theresa of Calcutta	St. Thérèse of Lisieux
Patrick Madrid	St. Francis de Sales
Scott Hahn	St. Alphonsus Liguori
Francis Fernandez	St. Augustine
St. Josemaria Escriva	St. Ignatius
Jacques Philippe	Josef Pieper
Brother Lawrence	Thomas Merton
Hannah Hurnard	St. Teresa of Avila
Fr. Walter Ciszek	Peter Kreeft
Dom Hubert Van Zeller	St. Thomas Aquinas
Fr. Thomas Dubay, S.M.	Any of the Saints
Father Jean Baptiste Saint-Jure	Any of the Popes
	Any of the Church Fathers

Digital Prayer Resources

New digital resources come and go every day, so, depending upon when you read this, it may not be up to date. Many of the websites have corresponding apps.

Catholic.com	3-minute-retreat
Universalis.com	LoyolaPress.com
Usccb.org	Catholic Study Bible (app)
StJosemaria.org	Bible (app)
RelevantRadio.com	Laudate (app)
Biblegateway.com	The Way (app)
Lighthousemedia.org	Hallow (app)
Franciscanmedia.org	Pray-as-you-go (podcast)
WordonFire.org	

Try it!

Which of these websites most appeals to you at this point? What about the apps?

Make a plan for how you will used 2 of these Christian resources.

–––––––––

What I like about _____ is:

Its type of Christian content is:

I will use it as often as:

–––––––––

What I like about _____ is:

Its type of Christian content is:

I will use it as often as:

Your Team

Who are the people that support you? There may be people you need to rely on more for some of these things. You have a team behind you and with you. Pray that God would show you who these people are. Write down names next to this list.

Someone...

...to cheer you up.

...to tell troubles.

...who will watch out for you.

...to teach you.

...a few steps ahead of you.

...you can encourage and help.

...who is on the path with Christ.

...who can pray with and for you.

...who challenges you.

Contact

It is very helpful to be in frequent communication with someone who is well established in the faith. Below are some people to whom you can reach out so that someone can walk along side of you for your encouragement.

Family- Is there anyone in your family to whom you feel close? Or, would like to be? There may be people of deep faith in your family- people with whom you could give and receive encouragement. The values your family teaches you are bedrock to who you are. Lean on its goodness.

Friends- Although you may not currently pray with any of your friends, this group is the one to look to for people who are at the same stage in life- who may have some of the same questions and needs as you.

Your local parish priests- Reach out to the priest in the Catholic church near you and let him know that you would like help in walking closely as a disciple of Jesus. There's a lot of variety in personalities so, don't stop here if you don't really get anywhere.

Fellowship of Catholic University Students- This group is amazing in its vision of spreading the good news by equipping people to become missionary disciples who help others to become disciples. They are primarily at colleges but they also serve the general public through a few parishes. Check them out at focus.org.

Masstimes.org- Getting to confession and Mass are crucial in being guided in the faith. This website can help you find Mass and Reconciliation times at any place in the country.

People in the pew- Be bold and get to know someone from church who seems a little older in the faith than you. Ask if they would like to be prayer partners with you for a season.

Religious Orders- Perhaps there is a religious order of monks, brothers or sisters near you. Attend some of their events or Masses and let them know that you are looking for guidance. It is worth getting to know some of this wonderful, motley crew.

My *Flexible* Plan

Write down the resources you will seek out. Help is there for you, friend! What are your curiosities? How can you grow? What grounding do you need?

What resources shall I use to aid me in a life of prayer?

❏ Classic prayer books:

❏ Digital resources:

❏ Authors for study:

❏ Christian friendship/mentor:

❏ Other ideas:

Dear God, I want to know and grow more by...

I am a person who is interested in...

Please send me...

Love,

Epilogue

I sit writing in front of a San Damiano crucifix. Jesus' arms are open wide and his head is high. By his side are saints and sinners, hiding behind his wounds. The halo of light surrounds his warming face. He welcomes me. Welcomes us. To join him. To forgiveness. To love. To suffering. To glory. To prayer.

I am incredibly thankful to Jesus for this Collection of Grace. The seeds contained in here have a grown life which bolsters me now in the midst of a difficult moment in history. Sometimes, it feels as if some of the treasures written here saved my life. However, these particular prayers, of course, are not "the answer". Jesus is. My friends show me this again and again. Sometimes I think I know a thing or two. And then, in my pride, I encounter a person whose life emits the flowers of true kindness, true humility – true flexibility – because her life is based on love. And God, the great gardener winks and tells me there is much, much more.

The path the Lord sets for us is unknown. But his desire to bless and grow us, his little children, is clear. He is desire to let our spirits to thrive is clear. Take his treasures. They are all around you. Receive his nourishment. He is already at work within you. May we all discover the life of prayer God is growing.

I am confident of this,
that the one who began a good work in you
will continue to complete it until the day of Christ Jesus.
-Philippians 1:6

Index

Index

Would you like to give this book to more than 10 people? Let me help! Contact me on the website: GraceFinders.com

Made in the USA
Monee, IL
29 October 2020